Clémence Cleave & Giovanna Torrico
Photography by Lisa Linder

28 Days
to Gut Health

**A practical guide to improve your
gut health and well-being**

Smith
Street
Books

Smith Street Books

First published in French by Hachette Livre, Marabout division
58, rue Jean-Bleuzen, 92178 Vanves Cedex, France

This Five Below edition published in 2024 by Smith Street Books | smithstreetbooks.com
Printed & bound in China by C&C Offset Printing Co., Ltd.

ISBN: 978-1-92304-967-3

All rights reserved. No part of this book may be reproduced or transmitted by any person or entity, in
any form or by any means, electronic or mechanical, including photocopying, recording, scanning or by
any storage and retrieval system, without the prior written permission of the publishers and copyright holders.

Copyright © Hachette Livre, Marabout division, 2022

Publisher: Paul McNally
Internal designer: Michelle Tilly
Cover designer: Murray Batten
Photographer: Lisa Linder
Stylist: Frankie Unsworth

FSC
www.fsc.org

MIX
Paper | Supporting
responsible forestry
FSC® C008047

Contents

Why Gut Health
Matters?

Have you ever had a gut feeling? Do you sometimes feel gutted? Or even gutsy? Instinctively, we have always known that the gut is more than just a digestive tube. Scientists even call it our second brain. But what's so unique about our gut and why does it matter?

The gut is at the core of well-being. Obviously, it is first and foremost the site where your digestion and nutrition happen: the food you eat is churned, broken down, absorbed, transformed and moved down the digestive tract to feed the body. But recent discoveries reveal that the gut plays many more roles in health and well-being: it interacts with your immune functions, communicates with your brain, affects your mood and regulates your energy levels and appetite. It is a fascinating system that is influenced by what you eat, your environment and your behavior.

1 **The large intestine**
It is easy to underestimate the large intestine (aka the colon). Long regarded as just a place for undigested food waste to linger before being pooped out, it is home to ill-smelling gases, an unpredictable appendix and more-or-less regular bowel movements. Then, in the 19th century, the concept of gut flora emerged. Scientists discovered that the gut was host to multiple microorganisms, some associated with good health, others with illness. But it is only in the last two decades, with the rise of genetic sequencing technology that scientists have started to realise the key roles that this internal ecosystem plays.

2 **Busy microbes**
Although the gut is inside you, it is actually an external organ, acting as the primary gateway into your body. With up to 4 lb of food eaten every day, there are lots of 'foreign' compounds trying to enter this portal. A bit like the door staff of a club, you need a reliable system to check what can safely be let in and what needs to be kept out. The gut microbes act as busy bouncers, making a physical barrier and constantly liaising with management (your brain) to protect you from undesirable visitors.

3 **When things go wrong**
Unfortunately, things can go wrong. If the gut microbiota is damaged – with the use of alcohol or antibiotics, for example, or with factors beyond our control – these lines of defense get weakened. Thankfully this is usually only temporary but in some cases, it can lead to chronic disorders or diseases (e.g. allergic reactions, lupus, Celiac disease, Crohn's disease, ulcerative colitis).

4 **Take care of your gut microbiota**
By nourishing and protecting your gut microbiota you can support your health and well-being. And what you eat matters: choosing a diet with lots of plant-based food rich in dietary fiber, polyphenols and fermented foods will help the gut microbiota flourish and thrive. Other aspects of life will also affect the gut microbiota: pollution, stress, medication, physical activity and sleep. In this book you will find lots of tasty recipes and useful health habits for taking care of your 'second brain'.

The digestive system

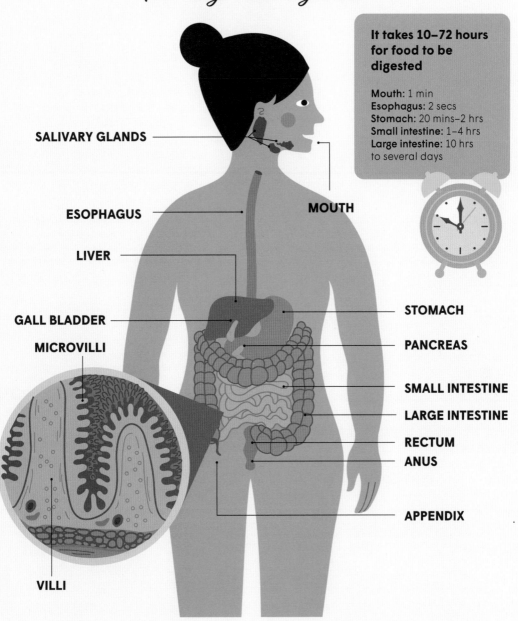

It takes 10–72 hours for food to be digested

Mouth: 1 min
Esophagus: 2 secs
Stomach: 20 mins–2 hrs
Small intestine: 1–4 hrs
Large intestine: 10 hrs
to several days

SALIVARY GLANDS

ESOPHAGUS

LIVER

GALL BLADDER

MICROVILLI

MOUTH

STOMACH

PANCREAS

SMALL INTESTINE

LARGE INTESTINE

RECTUM

ANUS

APPENDIX

VILLI

Understanding
Your Gut

Your digestive tract (aka the gut) is central to your body, literally.
It is 20 feet long, starting from the mouth and finishing with the anus. The
food you eat will take up to 72 hours to complete its journey through the gut,
during which a lot of action will take place.

① Digestion

It all starts in the mouth. Food gets broken down through actions both mechanical (by chewing and churning) and chemical (with enzyme and acid release) as it travels through the esophagus, the stomach and the small intestine.

→ Carbohydrates are transformed into simple sugar molecules.

→ Proteins are turned into small amino acids.

→ Fats are dispersed into tiny droplets.

→ Minerals and vitamins are set free, floating into the digestive tract.

This process is essential: it extracts the nutrients (ready for absorption) from the food, while the other food components can carry on their journey and finally get pooped out.

② Absorption

It is in the small intestine that most of the absorption happens. Here, broken-down food makes its way through 10–16 feet of tube with lots of folds covered in hair-like projections, called microvilli (a bit like a sea anemone) to increase its surface area and give more chance for nutrients to get across the gut wall into the body. Glucose molecules, amino acids and other water-soluble nutrients (some vitamins and minerals) join the bloodstream, while droplets of fats and vitamins A, D, E and K join the lymphatic system. After 2–6 hours, any unabsorbed nutrients and undigested food move further on, into the large intestine.

③ In the large intestine

Here, things slow right down – it can take more than two days for the food to travel only 5 feet. And here is where some true magic happens. The microorganisms that live in the large intestine start feasting on the food that hasn't been digested, releasing lots of compounds called metabolites (page 9):

→ B vitamins and vitamin K that then get absorbed

→ molecules that act as strong signals to the brain.

LIKE A DONUT!

Did you know that your gastrointestinal tract is in fact external to you? It is a long tube surrounded by the body in which food travels and gets churned, broken down, assimilated or discarded. Some have even compared the body to a donut where the gastrointestinal tract would be the hole in the middle.

Powerful Signaling

What goes on in the digestive tract affects the whole body. If the brain is command HQ, the gut is the secret intelligence that reports back, informing on the need for action from other organs. You should really trust your gut!

❶ Communication lines

The gut is constantly sending all kinds of signals via three main channels:

→ your nervous system

→ your immune system

→ your blood circulatory system.

Those signals target many organs: brain, liver, fat tissues, lungs, skin and muscles – all of which respond to the messages.

❷ Appetite ...

When the body needs energy but energy stores are down and the gut is empty, it sends a hormonal signal to the brain saying, 'it is time to eat'. When food is ingested and detected in the stomach, it sends a nerve signal to say, 'it feels like we are eating, nutrients coming soon!', which reassures the brain. And when nutrients finally reach the small intestine, satiety hormones are released saying to the brain and the liver, 'it looks like we have enough energy to sustain us for a while' – and this switches off your appetite.

❸ ... and beyond

The gut sends many signals that influence other aspects of your health. For example, it warns when the body is besieged by harmful pathogens and it informs your immune system about how hard it needs to fight back. It also modulates your experience of pain and sharpens your cognitive functions. It influences the levels of cholesterol in your bloodstream, it modulates your sensitivity to insulin and it affects your body fat accumulation.

Talkative microbes

It is the gut microbiota that is responsible for triggering and modulating many of these signals. Your colony of microbes stimulates the secretion of hormones (e.g. controlling hunger and satiety) and neurotransmitters (e.g. dopamine or serotonin). It can also prompt an immune response or an inflammation (e.g. skin rash) or send stress signals to the brain.

The Role of the
Gut Microbiome

Without your gut microbiome, you would get sick constantly, completely vulnerable to parasites and harmful bacteria. This is because your gut microbiome is a key component of your immune system. It also plays an important role in your nutrition – and may even modulate your mood.

1 First line of defense

The gut microbiome's main function is defense. First, by competing for space and limited resources in the gut, the microbiota prevents the overgrowth of pathogens that could threaten to invade your body. Certain strains in particular, like Lactobacillus and Bifidobacterium (often found in live yogurt) are useful because they will inhibit the growth of less desirable bacteria.

Another way your gut microbiome acts as a defense is by interacting with your immune system. It constantly assesses what is traveling through your digestive tract and sends signals to the immune cells advising on:

→ what can safely be let in through your gut barrier

→ what can happily be tolerated in the gut

→ what actually requires a proper immune response, and how strong this response needs to be.

In other words, the gut microbiome trains your immune system to tell friends from foes and then shapes your immune responses.

2 Nutrition

The gut microbiome's other important job is to extract and synthesize more interesting nutrients from the food you eat. By breaking down dietary fiber (a carbohydrate found in plants that we humans can't digest) your bacteria produce essential vitamins like vitamin K and folate, which can then be absorbed. It also facilitates the absorption of minerals such as magnesium, iron and calcium. And finally, it produces some mighty compounds called short-chain fatty acids. When released in the gut, these:

→ strengthen the gut barrier by nourishing the mucous layer of the gut wall – a process that is suspected to reduce the risk of colorectal cancer

→ get absorbed, sending signals to the brain, thus regulating hunger long after your meal.

3 Mood & behaviors

Did you know that your gut bacteria produce neurotransmitters like dopamine and serotonin? In fact, 95 per cent of serotonin – sometimes called the 'happiness hormone' – is secreted in the gut. Serotonin in the gut plays an important role in gut motility (i.e. the speed at which foods travel through the gut) but it also targets the area in the brain involved in mood regulation and cognition. For example, it might affect your experience of stress, your social interactions, your memory and concentration. This is referred to as the gut–brain axis.

What is a Healthy
Gut Microbiota?

There isn't one ideal microbiome. They come in all kinds, and what is healthy for you might not be right for someone else. But a few characteristics such as stability, size and diversity appear to be key.

1 Stability

Microbes interact with each other, creating a fine balance. Certain strains are particularly beneficial, for example, Bifidobacterium or Lactobacillus found in live yogurt; while others are potentially dangerous (Clostridium difficile, E. coli). But it would be over-simplistic to say that there are 'bad' bacteria that need to be eliminated. Imagine a sea where there were only plankton and no sharks – it wouldn't work! What is crucial here is stability and equilibrium. Like any ecosystem, all the organisms work together to keep the microbiota stable and optimal for the host – you!

2 Size matters

The bigger the microbiota, the less space there is for harmful microbes to take over and cause damage. A large microbiota seems to improve the whole stability of the ecosystem – the more the merrier!

3 Diversity

A wide range of microbes makes your gut microbiome more capable and resilient. This is because it means a greater diversity in skills: all these microbes produce different metabolites that work for you, doing all kinds of different things. A bit like an organization, we need all kinds of workers who can be deployed to fight, protect, investigate and strategize. In this community too, diversity is a strength!

4 Shaping your microbiome

Your microbiome is shaped by many factors. Some are out of your control – your genes, your age, the way you were born, infections you've had in the past. But some lifestyle factors may be more within your power: living with pets, spending time in nature, sleeping well and exercising regularly are all beneficial. And obviously, what you eat has a direct and powerful effect on the size, diversity and stability of your microbiome. That's where this book can come in handy!

WHAT ARE METABOLITES?

Small molecules produced from the breakdown – the metabolism – of food or drugs. Metabolites can be nutrients, vitamins, fatty acids, phenols, etc. The digestive system as well as the microbes in the gut produce metabolites, which can then be absorbed by the body or act as signals to other organs.

Foods for a Thriving
Gut Microbiota

By following a few simple principles and tweaking your diet, you can do wonders for your gut and its residents. A great way to start is by adding more plants to your plate.

1 Plants, more plants

Let's be clear: there's no need to go vegan, at least as far as gut health is concerned, but it's worth focusing on bringing more plants to your plate. This is because the microorganisms that live in your gut LOVE them. In particular, they love dietary fiber. Fiber is a type of carbohydrate found in plants, but unlike other carbs (sugar, starch) your body is unable to break it down – you just don't have the right enzyme to digest and extract energy from it. The good news though: your gut microbiota can, and they do! They feast on fiber, fuelling their growth in numbers.

2 Even more plants

It is not only fiber that is good in plants, there are also phytochemicals ('phyto' meaning from plants) with antioxidative properties. These polyphenols stimulate the growth of the right kind of microorganisms and also strengthen the gut barrier.

3 Some fermented foods

If dietary fiber is considered the 'fertilizer' for gut microorganisms, fermented foods are the 'seeds'. Fermented foods such as yogurt and sauerkraut are full of live bacteria. By eating these foods some bacteria will reach your colon and settle there, adding more volume and diversity to your gut microbiota.

4 A bit of interesting fat

Omega-3, a type of polyunsaturated fat, is particularly good because it increases the quantity of beneficial bacteria known for their ability to produce short-chain fatty acids and positively stimulate the gut–brain axis. Omega-3 fat can be found in oily fish (e.g. salmon, mackerel, sardines, tuna, trout), as well as in plant-based foods like walnuts, flax seeds and chia seeds. Finally, don't forget olive oil. This monounsaturated fat also does wonders for your gut.

5 Stay hydrated

It is not only food that keeps the gut microbiota in good shape, water is also important, lowering the numbers of potentially harmful bacteria and creating the perfect conditions for your ecosystem to thrive.

The Benefits of
Dietary Fiber

Fiber, the non-digestible carbohydrate found in plants, is key to a happy gut. But there isn't just one kind of fiber – there are over 100. Different fibers have very different health effects and functions.

❶ Poop regulation

Soluble fiber dissolves slowly in the gut creating a thick, jelly-like texture. This slows down the digestion and will help with creating the perfect poop: not too runny, not too hard. It is also associated with lower levels of cholesterol and better blood glucose levels. It is found in oats, barley, beans, lentils, peas and apples.

Insoluble fiber adds bulk to the stool, speeding up the passing of food through the gut. It gets things moving! It is found in the skin of fruit and vegetables, in wholegrains, seeds and nuts.

❷ Fascinating fermentation

Some fibers, such as resistant starch, are highly fermentable, which means that they get broken down by the gut microbiota – it is their fuel. Not only do such fibers enable the microbes to thrive but, through the process of fermentation, they produce something wonderful: short-chain fatty acids. These metabolites are the ingredient for good health beyond the gut: they modulate the immune function, influence hormone secretion and stimulate the nervous system.

Fermentable fiber is found in potatoes, green bananas, wholegrains, pulses, legumes, cashew nuts and oats.

❸ The more the better – but not any old how

The current recommendation is to aim for at least 1 oz of fiber per day, yet currently the average adult gets only about half that daily. There is clearly room for improvement! Better health results have been associated with a much higher amount of dietary fiber (around 1¾ oz a day).

However, there are two precautions when increasing the amount of fiber in your diet:

→ First, fiber should be added gradually to allow the gut to adjust to these changes. Otherwise, the sudden feast in the large intestine might come with some discomfort such as bloating and gas.

→ Second, since some fiber will draw a lot of water into the gut, it is important to increase your hydration to avoid cramps.

DID YOU KNOW?

Plant skin is a great source of fiber, so don't peel everything. Banana skin might not be to everyone's taste, but do keep the skin on apples, cucumbers, eggplant and sweet potatoes.

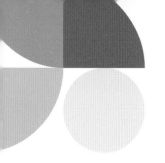

Diversity First
& Foremost

Different types of fiber feed different microorganisms. This means that a diet with a broad range of plants will lead to greater diversity of microbes in the gut. And the greater the gut microbiota diversity, the better the gut health. So, why not try something new?

❶ The 30-plant challenge

Research from the American Gut Microbiome project showed that people who ate more than 30 different plant-based foods per week had a much more diverse gut microbiota compared to those who ate less than 10 plants per week. So, are you ready for the 30-plant challenge? It is much easier than it sounds. Think of fruit, vegetables, wholegrains, nuts, seeds, pulses, herbs and spices. It all counts!

❷ Here are some ideas: Easy add-ons

Having cereal for breakfast? Top it with a few berries and nuts.

Snacking on an apple? Chop it and dip it into the nut butter of your choice.

Eating a sandwich for lunch? Tuck in a few leaves of arugula.

Serving soup for dinner? Scatter some seeds and herbs on top.

Planning to roast some vegetables? Season them with various spices (cumin, smoked paprika, ground turmeric).

Making a bolognese for the family? Halve the amount of meat and add some lentils or beans instead. Add some sweet potato and zucchini for good measure.

❸ Easy swaps

Always eating the same white bread? Swap for wholegrain and vary the grain: how about trying rye or spelt?

Regularly snacking on cashew nuts? Swap for almonds or walnuts.

Broccoli is your go-to vegetable? Try Romanesco broccoli or cauliflower.

Eating a lot of rice? Try brown, wild, black or red rice.

Making chicken schnitzels? Swap the breadcrumbs for milled oats or crushed cereal.

Check out the recipes in this book (pages 26–111). They are full of fiber-packed foods, using different grains, a wide variety of nuts and seeds and lots of herb toppings so you should easily eat 30 different plants a week, and more!

LET'S GO

Try the 30-plant challenge

VEGETABLES

Artichokes
Asparagus
Beets
Bell peppers
Brussels sprouts
Broccoli
Butternut squash
Carrots
Cauliflower
Eggplant
French shallots
Garlic
Green beans
Hispi cabbage
Leeks
Olives
Parsnips
Pumpkin
Red onions
Rutabaga
Siberian kale
Spinach
Spring greens
Sweet potatoes
Sweetcorn
Tomatoes
Turnips
Yellow zucchini

FRUIT

Apples
Apricots
Bananas
Blueberries
Cantaloupe
Cherries
Grapefruit
Kiwi fruit
Mangoes
Peaches
Pears
Plums
Pomegranates
Red grapes
Strawberries

WHOLEGRAINS

Amaranth
Barley
Brown rice
Buckwheat
Bulgur
Freekeh
Kamut wheat
Millet
Oats
Quinoa
Red rice
Rye
Spelt
Wholemeal wheat
Wild rice

LEGUMES

Beluga lentils
Black beans
Black-eyed peas
Cannellini beans
Cranberry beans
Garbanzo beans
Kidney beans
Lupin beans
Mung beans
Peanuts
Pinto beans
Puy lentils
Red lentils
Soy beans
Split peas

HERBS & SPICES

Basil
Chives
Cilantro
Dill
Lemongrass
Mint
Oregano
Parsley
Rosemary
Tarragon
Thyme

Black pepper
Cardamom
Chili
Cinnamon
Coriander seed
Cumin
Ginger
Mustard
Nutmeg
Smoked paprika
Turmeric

NUTS & SEEDS

Almonds
Brazil nuts
Cashews
Chia seeds
Hazelnuts
Flax seeds
Macadamias
Pistachios
Pumpkin seeds
Sesame seeds
Sunflower seeds
Walnuts

Prebiotics,
food for our gut microbes

Although all types of dietary fiber are great for your gut, make sure
you specifically include the best ones – the ones that good bacteria
(i.e. the ones known to have health benefits) love to feed on. These are
called prebiotics (not to be confused with probiotics – more on those later).

1 Some mighty fibers

All prebiotics are fibers, but not all dietary fibers
are prebiotics. To be a prebiotic, the fiber needs
to be fermentable – in other words it needs
to be edible by the gut microbes. Secondly, it
needs to be proven to modify, for the better, the
composition and function of the gut microbiota.
Currently, the main prebiotics that have been
identified are inulin, oligofructose (OF),
galacto-oligosaccharides (GOS) and fructo-
oligosaccharides (FOS). You might see these
names mentioned on gut-friendly foods' labels.

2 Health benefits

Prebiotics are an easy way to support our health.
They are thought to help with digestion, appetite
regulation, blood glucose levels, immune
function and mineral absorption. They may also
help with mood regulation, cognitive functions
(memory and learning) and stress management.
Interestingly, a lot of prebiotics are present in
breast milk and play a key role in supporting
a newborn's health, right from the beginning.

3 Prebiotic-rich foods

Prebiotics can be found in a wide range of fruit,
vegetables, grains, nuts and legumes. Here are
some great sources:
- → **Vegetables:** asparagus, chicory root,
  Jerusalem artichokes, leeks, onions, garlic
- → **Fruit:** dried figs, dried mango, apricots,
  green bananas, prunes, nectarines
- → **Grains:** oats, barley, rye, spelt
- → **Nuts:** almonds, cashew nuts, pistachios,
  hazelnuts
- → **Legumes:** black beans, garbanzo beans,
  lima beans.

4 Go slow

Like any fiber, it is important to introduce
prebiotics progressively in the diet to avoid
discomfort such as gas or bloating. The body –
and the gut microbiota – need a bit of time
to adapt to this change in diet.

5 How about a pill?

You might have seen prebiotics offered as food
supplements, but it is currently not very clear
how helpful they are. The best strategy by far
is to focus on prebiotic-rich foods, as this will
certainly be celebrated in your gut.

Fermented
Foods

Fermentation has been around for thousands of years as a technique to preserve food and increase its shelf life. But wait, there's much more to it!

1 The fermentation process

The principle of lacto-fermentation is simple: by stimulating the growth of harmless yeast or bacteria in an airtight container it inhibits the proliferation of pathogens and prevents the food from spoiling. What happens in the sauerkraut jar is very much like what happens in your gut. The bacteria feed on the carbohydrates (fiber for kimchi, milk for yogurt) and multiply, breaking down food molecules and producing by-products like gas and bio-active compounds such as lactic acid and vitamins.

2 Delicious & highly digestible

This transformation improves the texture and the taste of the food, giving a sour, tangy and sometimes even fizzy flavor. It also changes the molecular structure of the food. For example, the lactose molecules in yogurt (or in fermented cheese) are broken down by the bacteria making it much more digestible for people with lactose intolerance. It is the same with sourdough bread: because of its fermentation, it is often much better tolerated by wheat-sensitive people. It also enhances the nutrition value of the food through the synthesis of vitamins and other biologically active molecules.

3 Sowing the seeds

Fermented foods, as long as they haven't been cooked or pasteurized, are a great source of live microorganisms. By eating live microbes – a bit like sowing seeds in a garden – some will flourish in your gut, adding volume and diversity to your existing gut microbiota.

4 What to eat

To give your gut microbiota a boost, choose foods that have retained their live microbes (check for 'live culture' on the label):

→ yogurt, kefir, cheese
→ sauerkraut, kimchi and other lacto-fermented (pickled) vegetables
→ drinks, such as kombucha, some beers
→ fermented soy products, such as miso, natto, tempeh.

Fermented foods that are cooked or pasteurized won't have any live microorganisms any more but will have retained their higher digestibility:

→ sourdough bread
→ wine, most beers
→ soy sauce
→ coffee and chocolate beans.

The Power
of Colors

Besides dietary fiber, there is another family of components from plant food that's worth paying attention to: polyphenols. These bio-active phytochemicals are often praised for their antioxidant properties. They also appear to modulate the activity of our gut microbiota for the better.

1 Eat the rainbow

Resveratrol from red wine and raspberries, curcuma from turmeric, flavanols from cocoa and tea, tannins from tea and coffee, anthocyanins from berries and red cabbage … there are hundreds of polyphenols in nature, often linked to the tastes, aromas and colors of the plants. Hence, the importance of eating foods of all different colors. They are widely found in fruit, vegetables, legumes, herbs, seeds and spices.

2 Health benefits

Scientists think that these polyphenols may have powerful protective effects against diseases such as diabetes, obesity, neurodegenerative disorders, cardiovascular diseases and even certain cancers. But how could they work?

3 The role of the gut microbiome

Only a small amount of polyphenols is absorbed during digestion in the small intestine. The bulk of them gets broken down by the gut microbiota in the colon, a process which produces lots of active metabolites (page 9). It is these metabolites that will have anti-inflammatory, anti-allergenic and anticarcinogenic effects, so, bring colors to your plate!

4 Shaping the microbiota too

The presence of these polyphenols will also influence the composition of your gut microbiota: they stimulate the growth of the beneficial microbes while keeping under control the proliferation of the more harmful ones. By having lots of polyphenol-rich food in your diet, you really strengthen the balance, size and stability of your gut microbiome.

TIP

Light stimulates the production of polyphenols so they are often concentrated in the outer layer, such as the skin and leaves. This is another good reason not to peel fruit and vegetables, and to sprinkle your plate with lots of fresh herbs.

Flavanones
These may help with inflammation in the body and help protect it against toxins. They are found in lemons, grapefruits and oranges.

Anthocyanins
These are usually found in the outer skin of fruit and vegetables including pomegranates, red cabbage, red onions, blueberries, radishes and eggplants.

Isoflavones
These are also known as phytoestrogens (they are similar in structure to estrogen) and are found in soy beans, apricots, mangoes, plums and sesame seeds.

Phenolic acids
These may have anti-inflammatory properties and are found in a wide range of plant-based foods including strawberries, blackberries, tea, onions and tomatoes.

Flavanols
These have antioxidant properties and may help lower blood pressure and can manage symptoms of cardiovascular disease. They are found in broccoli, curly kale, leeks, apples and green tea.

Probiotics,
your gut's good guys

Some bacteria turn out to be particularly helpful, healthwise, and can be found in some fermented foods or in food supplements. Are you ready to give them a go?

1 Probiotic-containing foods

A lot of fermented foods such as kefir, live yogurt and kimchi will contain amounts of these beneficial live microorganisms – and yet, they may not be called probiotics. This is because products need to meet three rigorous criteria:

→ The microbes need to be alive.

→ The strains need to have documented health benefits.

→ They must be present in large amounts.

So, if the kefir from the supermarket doesn't say 'probiotic', this doesn't mean that it won't have any health benefit – rather, the manufacturer wasn't able to guarantee that the three criteria were met. They are producing food, after all, not medicine.

2 Probiotics as supplements

You can also find probiotics as food supplements. These can certainly be useful, especially when:

→ you take them alongside a course of antibiotics

→ you have gut issues such as irritable bowel syndrome (IBS), diarrhea, or you are at risk of inflammatory bowel disease (Crohn's disease, ulcerative colitis)

→ you are healthy but want to prevent some illnesses.

Probiotics are considered safe to use by adults but do check with a healthcare professional if you are pregnant, have a compromised immune system, or would like to use them for a child.

3 Be strategic

Here are a few things to keep in mind:

→ Different strains will have different health benefits, so be specific when choosing your probiotic and ask for help from a healthcare professional.

→ Not all probiotics will have been clinically tested: the right strains might be present in large amounts, but will they arrive in sufficient numbers in the gut? Choose a reliable brand and check if it has been properly tested.

→ Not everyone will get benefits from the same probiotic – the microbiome is still a big, unknown field, and it is hard to know what will have an effect or not.

DEFINITION

Probiotic (not to be confused with 'prebiotic', page 14) is the name given to any live microorganism that, when taken in adequate amounts, has been shown to provide health benefits. They may help with diarrhea, constipation or bloating; with irritable bowel symptoms and managing cholesterol levels.

7 benefits of good gut bacteria

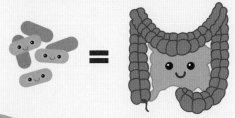

Gut barrier
Protects and strengthens the gut wall, which may prevent inflammation and some types of cancers.

pH levels
Reduces slightly the pH levels in the colon and prevents infections.

Harmful invaders
Can prevent bad bacteria invading the body through the gut.

Immune function
Trains the immune system on how to respond to pathogens.

Diarrhea
May help to relieve the occurrence and duration of diarrhea caused by illness or antibiotics.

Nutrition
Helps with extracting more nutrients from the food you have eaten.

IBS symptoms
Can help to reduce bloating, abdominal pain and improve stool shape in people with IBS.

Basic, Snack & Drink
Recipes

WITH

- Ingredients you need to cook healthy recipes
- How to make kimchi & lacto-fermented pickles
- How to make live yogurt
- How to sprout seeds & pulses easily

Storecupboard
ingredients

It can be difficult to know what to eat to support your gut, but the reality is that many of the foods we already have in the cupboard are ingredients that can be considered the basis of a gut-healthy diet. Pulses, grains, nuts, seeds and spices offer fiber, which can help support our digestive system, as well as prebiotics and other important nutrients.

Pulses & grains

Pulses and grains are staples in diets all over the world. Pulses are a great source of protein, healthy carbohydrates, several vitamins, calcium, zinc and potassium. They offer an excellent nutrition package and help to stabilise blood sugar, preventing and managing type 2 diabetes. They are also powerful antioxidants and have anti-inflammatory properties. Whole grains offer a complete package of health benefits, unlike refined ones. It is good to plan ahead and cook pulses and grains, then freeze them in batches.

Nuts & seeds

Nuts and seeds are packed with micronutrients and healthy fats. They can help keep you fuller for longer and are among the best sources of plant-based proteins. It is always handy to keep a good selection in your pantry as quick snacks or as enhancers to different recipes.

Spices

Spices play a significant role in the way we cook and consume food. They provide a depth of flavor to any dish and are known to have several health benefits.

Flours

Flour is a pantry staple used for both savory and sweet recipes. Some are healthier than others and it is good to replace white flour with more wholesome options. Interestingly, some flours aren't actually made from grains but from nuts or seeds, such as almond, buckwheat, quinoa and flax seeds.

Oil

The health benefits of extra virgin olive oil are unequalled, from its anti-inflammatory properties to reduction of heart and diabetes problems. It is the cornerstone of the Mediterranean diet and is naturally high in healthy fatty acids. Rapeseed oil is a great source of some omega-3 fats and as it has a high smoke point, it makes it a good choice for frying or roasting.

Condiments

Kimchi, pickle and pesto are only a few examples of adding condiments to your meals to enhance flavor and also add health benefits.

Protein &
dairy products

Research shows that fiber-rich foods can help gut microbes to flourish, but a balanced diet needs to include protein-rich foods. For example, live yogurt contains beneficial probiotics; beans and pulses are filled with prebiotics and fiber; and tempeh and tofu are perfect plant-based proteins to eat for your gut as an alternative to meat.

Eggs

Eggs are an important and versatile ingredient for cooking. They are rich in nutrients, including proteins, vitamins and minerals. The yolk contains fat-soluble vitamins (such as vitamins D and E) and essential fatty acids, while most of the protein is found in the egg white.

Fish

Fish is an easy and nutritious way to add vitamins and minerals to your diet and makes a great high-protein alternative to red meat and poultry. It is recommended to eat at least one portion per week of oily fish, such as salmon, mackerel, anchovies or sardines, as they contain omega-3 fats.

Meat

A healthy balanced diet can include protein from meat such as chicken, lamb and beef. When buying meat you should always go for the leanest option.

Pulses

Pulses are also an important plant-based source of protein. The amount of protein in lentils, beans, garbanzo beans and peas is 2–3 times the levels found in grains like quinoa, oats or barley.

Tofu

Soy products, like tofu, are powerful antioxidants. Tofu is a popular plant-based meat and dairy alternative and a rich source of protein, providing all nine essential amino acids we need for growth, repair and functions like immunity. It also contains vitamins and minerals including calcium as well as beneficial isoflavones or phytoestrogens (page 17). It can be cooked in many different ways, from stir-fries to marinated and baked.

Tempeh

Made from fermented soy beans, tempeh is a nutrient-dense, plant-based ingredient rich in protein, which is also known for its filling and satiating effect. It is rich in fiber, the type known to be prebiotic, that feeds the beneficial bacteria in the gut. It is higher in protein than tofu, and is less processed. Tempeh is very versatile in cooking: add it to stir-fries with vegetables and brown rice, marinate it, fry it and add it to your favorite bowl recipe.

Milk, cheese & yogurt

Dairy products like milk, cheese and yogurt are rich in protein and contain many essential vitamins and minerals, including calcium and magnesium, as well as supplying all the essential amino acids that our body needs. Regular yogurt consumption can help to improve gut bacteria and decrease symptoms of lactose intolerance. It is always best to opt for natural, unsweetened yogurt that is made just from milk and contains live bacteria, which are sometimes called 'starter cultures'. Additionally, to reap the gut health benefits, make sure the label reads: 'contains live active cultures'.

Fruit
& vegetables

The easiest way to ensure a healthy gut is by eating plenty of fruit and vegetables that are high in fiber and promote a proper intestinal balance. Vegetables are the best source of nutrients for a healthy gut microbiome. Soups are a great way to consume multiple servings of vegetables at once, and because the leafy greens wilt easily and reduce in size, they are the perfect vegetables for tossing into pasta and making sauces.

Bananas

Bananas are high in fiber, which can help keep you feeling fuller for longer, lower cholesterol and may reduce bloating. As they contain a prebiotic fiber, bananas can help to feed your gut's bacteria to improve digestive health and boost your immune system. One medium banana provides approximately 10 per cent of a person's fiber needs for a day. Bananas are also rich in potassium, which may lower blood pressure and protect against heart disease.

Berries

Berries, like blueberries, blackberries and raspberries, are among the healthiest foods we can eat to help diversify our gut bacteria. They contain high levels of antioxidants, which may protect our cells from free radical damage, as well as enough plentiful fiber, which may increase the feeling of fullness. Berries are also low in calories but rich in lots of vitamins and minerals like vitamin C and manganese.

Other fruits

Kiwi fruit is a fat-free, nutrient-dense source of energy. The skin of pears contains 3–4 times as many phenolic phytonutrients, like antioxidants, as the flesh. Apples are an incredibly nutritious fruit that offer multiple health benefits, rich in fiber and antioxidants. They can also reduce the risk of many chronic conditions such as diabetes, heart disease and cancer and improve gut and brain health.

Leafy greens

Leafy greens, such as spinach, kale and Swiss chard, play an important role in a healthy diet. They are excellent sources of fiber, packed with different types of vitamins and minerals, including vitamin K, iron and calcium, but are also low in calories. A diet rich in leafy greens can offer numerous health benefits including a reduced risk of obesity, heart disease and high blood pressure.

Brassicas

Most vegetables are naturally high in fiber, but the brassica or cruciferous family, such as broccoli and cauliflower, gets a gold star. They also contain high levels of carotenoid, vitamins C and K, folate, manganese and potassium. When shopping, avoid any vegetable that shows signs of aging and always choose the crispest and greenest type. It is also important not to overcook brassicas in order not to lose all their benefits.

Garlic, onions & leeks

Garlic, onions, leeks and French shallots stimulate the growth of beneficial microbiota. Due to its antibacterial, antifungal and antiviral properties, garlic is known to reduce inflammation and lower high blood pressure, while onions can normalise digestion and leeks are rich in antioxidants and sulfur compounds. Leeks are also a good source of soluble fiber, which feeds the beneficial bacteria in your gut, and these bacteria reduce inflammation and promote digestive health.

Potatoes & Jerusalem artichokes

Also high on the prebiotic list is the resistant starch found in potatoes and Jerusalem artichokes, while artichokes, chicory (endive), asparagus and carrots are rich in polyphenols.

Herbs

Herbs, like spices, can elevate dishes from dull to delicious and it turns out that they are also important for gut health. They can help with digestive function and support the gut's ability to break down food. Herbs such as rosemary, sage, oregano and peppermint are excellent sources of antioxidants with their high content of phenolic compounds (see page 17).

Classic Kimchi

Kimchi is the national food of South Korea. It is crunchy and flavorsome, and with its vitamins, minerals and antioxidants, it can provide impressive health benefits. As with all fermented food, kimchi is an excellent probiotic and contains the same Lactobacilli bacteria found in yogurt and other fermented foods. Spicy and sour, kimchi can be eaten by itself or used in cooking to flavor stews, noodles and salads – just add it after cooking to preserve its good bacteria.

MAKES: 1 LB 11 OZ
PREPARATION: 6 DAYS
COOK: 0 MINUTES

1 large Chinese or napa cabbage, quartered and chopped to desired thickness
2 oz sea salt
3½ oz carrot, grated
1 bunch scallions, cut into 1 inch slices
3½ oz daikon radish, peeled and cut into matchsticks
1 tablespoon soy sauce
½ tablespoon grated garlic
1 teaspoon grated ginger
1 teaspoon chili powder
1 teaspoon paprika

Put cabbage and salt into a large bowl and massage the salt into the cabbage. Cover with 8 cups water and leave to soak overnight. Next day, drain and rinse cabbage a few times to get rid of excess salt, then squeeze out any water and put into a large bowl. Add all remaining ingredients and mix well. Transfer mixture to a sterilized 4-cup capacity jar, pressing down firmly until liquid rises to cover vegetables. Seal jar with lid and leave it to ferment for 5 days. Taste kimchi once a day, opening jar and pressing vegetables down to keep them covered with liquid. Once it has reached your preferred flavor, transfer to a sterilized smaller jar, squash down well, seal with a lid and chill in fridge for up to 9 months. You can eat it immediately, but it is better to leave it for another 2 weeks to allow flavors to develop.

make it happen

Live Yogurt

Live yogurt has been fermented with live cultures or friendly bacteria that are considered good for the digestive system. It contains nearly every nutrient that your body needs and also high amounts of calcium, which helps with the health of your teeth and bones. Help to balance the natural bacteria in your gut by trying to regularly include live yogurt into your diet: add it to fresh fruit in the morning, dollop it in soup or use it as an ingredient in baking.

MAKES: 1½ CUPS
PREPARATION: 13 HOURS
COOK: 15 MINUTES

2 cups whole milk
1¾ oz natural yogurt

Pour milk into a very clean saucepan and bring to the boil. Lower heat slightly and simmer for 15 minutes, stirring constantly, until milk is reduced by a quarter. Pour milk into a sterilized glass container, leave to cool to 113°F, then stir in yogurt. Cover with a plate and leave in a cold oven, with the light on, for 8–12 hours. Remove from the oven to cool before storing in the fridge for up to a week.

Sprouting Seeds & Pulses

Recently, the process of sprouting has become more popular and this is because eating sprouted seeds, pulses and grains, unlocks vital benefits. Sprouts contain vitamins C and B and proteins, and the process breaks down enzyme inhibitors so the body can easily absorb minerals. Their firm, crunchy texture is good for stir-fries as well as salads, as a topping for dips and broths or as a sprinkle on top of a bowl of noodles. Only use seeds, lentils or beans that are intended for sprouting, and if your sprouts go brown or have a sour smell, then discard them. Make sure all your equipment, including your jars, are sterilized before using.

MAKES: 1¾ OZ
PREPARATION: 7 DAYS
COOK: 45 MINUTES

1¾ oz alfalfa, broccoli, dried peas, lentils or garbanzo beans, specifically for home sprouting

Rinse and drain seeds or pulses, then put them into a clean mason jar, cover with 5 fl oz cool water and stir to make sure all seeds are wet. Cover top with a piece of cheesecloth secured with an elastic band or string and leave to soak overnight at room temperature. Next morning, using a sieve, strain seeds or pulses, then rinse and drain seeds or pulses again and put back into jar. To remove all excess water, put jar upside down in a bowl at a 45-degree angle to drain. Repeat same process in evening, then again for next 5 days, or until you get sprout length you want. Rinse sprouts again, drain and pat dry before putting them into an airtight sterilized jar ready to be stored in fridge. For pulses, simmer for 45 minutes before doing same process as for seeds. Store in fridge for up to 5 days.

 **CHEERS**

Triple Nut Butter

Nuts are low in carbohydrates and loaded with heart-healthy monounsaturated fats. They also have plenty of nutrients, such as vitamin E, magnesium and potassium, as well as selenium and manganese. A serving of nut butter is a great source of valuable nutrients. Homemade nut butter is easy to make and allows you to create your own blends. Nut butter is a versatile ingredient, you can stir it into porridge, use it as a base for muffins or cakes, add it to smoothies, spread it on toast, eat it with fresh fruit for an additional nutrient punch, or stir it into sauces for added flavor.

MAKES: 1 LB 5 OZ
PREPARATION: 5 MINUTES
COOK: 12 MINUTES

1 lb mixed almonds, walnuts, hazelnuts
3½ fl oz coconut oil, melted
3 Medjool dates, pitted
pinch of salt

Preheat oven to 375°F. Arrange nuts on a lined baking tray in a single layer and bake for 12 minutes. Remove and leave to cool completely. Blitz nuts with oil, dates and salt in a blender, stopping to scrape down as necessary, until mixture is completely smooth. If it is too dry add some water. Store in an airtight glass container in fridge for up to 3 weeks.

Super Seedy & Multigrain Granola

Granola is a very popular breakfast ingredient. While store-bought ones may be cheaper, making your own gives you control on prioritizing wholegrains rather than refined sugar and palm oil. Wholegrains, such as oats, contain prebiotic fiber, which may increase the levels of healthy gut bacteria compared to cereals made with refined grains. This homemade version is full of protein-rich nuts and seeds as well as a small amount of honey and salt. There are plenty of ways to enjoy granola from sprinkling it onto yogurt or ice cream, baking with it or eating it as a snack.

MAKES: 1 LB 4 OZ
PREPARATION: 5 MINUTES
COOK: 20 MINUTES

5½ oz jumbo oats
5½ oz grain of choice (spelt, barley, rye)
2¾ oz mixed seeds
2¾ oz mixed nuts, roughly chopped
pinch of salt
3 tablespoons coconut oil
1¾ fl oz honey
⅓ cup coconut flakes

Preheat oven to 300°F. Put oats, grain, mixed seeds, nuts and salt into a large bowl and mix well to combine. Heat oil and honey together in a small saucepan for 1 minute, whisking thoroughly. Pour over the dry ingredients and stir to coat evenly. Spread mix out on a lined baking tray and bake for 10 minutes. Add coconut flakes and bake for another 10 minutes. Leave to cool before transferring to an airtight container. Store for up to 2 weeks.

Lacto-fermented Pickles

Lacto-fermentation is a type of fermentation that uses lactic-acid-producing bacteria to preserve foods while adding flavor, texture and aroma. It is a process that increases the nutritional value of food and makes vegetables easier to digest. Pickles are also rich in nutrients and good for the microbiota. Every vegetable can be fermented, and they are perfect for snacking on or adding to a meal for a probiotic boost as well as a flavor enhancer.

MAKES: 1 LB
PREPARATION: 2 DAYS
COOK: 0 MINUTES

1 lb carrot, broccoli, radish or
   cucumber
½ oz sea salt
¼ teaspoon black peppercorns
1 bay leaf
1 garlic clove, chopped

Wash a 4-cup capacity mason jar with hot soapy water and rinse well. Chop or slice vegetables of your choice. Put salt and 1½ cups water into a large bowl and stir until salt has dissolved. Put all vegetables, peppercorns, bay leaf and garlic into the clean jar, pour in salty water and press down with a clean rolling pin until juice comes to the top, leaving about 1 inch. Add more water, if necessary, to cover vegetables. Make sure vegetables are submerged. Cover jar tightly with lid and leave to stand at room temperature for 2 days. After 2 days, open jar to taste pickles and to release gases produced during fermentation. When pickles taste to your liking, transfer jar to fridge and eat within a month.

Drinks

Sometimes it is good to alternate coffee with other non-caffeinated drinks. Try kombucha, a mildly fizzy fermented drink, rich in probiotics and antioxidants, or a refreshing tonic made with ginger and turmeric packed with antioxidants that help to cleanse your body and strengthen your immune system.

KOMBUCHA TEA

MAKES: 4 CUPS
PREPARATION: 7–14 DAYS
COOK: 5 MINUTES

2 teaspoons loose-leaf black tea
3½ oz granulated sugar
1 SCOBY (symbiotic culture
    of bacteria and yeast)

Put leaf tea into a 5-cup capacity heatproof glass jar. Bring 4 cups water and sugar to the boil in a large saucepan, then pour over the tea, cover with cheesecloth and leave overnight. Next day, strain tea into another large jar and add SCOBY. Cover jar with cheesecloth, so SCOBY can breathe, and secure it with an elastic band. Leave to ferment in a warm room out of direct sunlight for 7–14 days. Try a sample every 2 days until it reaches your desired flavor, then remove SCOBY and 7–8½ fl oz starter liquid for next batch. Pour kombucha into sterilized glass bottles and store in fridge. Kombucha is ready to drink immediately or add flavorings, such as fruit, herbs and spices, then ferment for another 2 days in fridge. Use SCOBY for up to a month at room temperature resting in some kombucha.

LEMONGRASS, GINGER & TURMERIC TONIC

MAKES: 1 CUP
PREPARATION: 5 MINUTES
COOK: 10 MINUTES

½ inch piece ginger, peeled
½ lemongrass stalk, outer leaves
    removed, halved lengthways
1 inch piece turmeric root or
    1 tablespoon ground turmeric
splash of tonic water
juice of 1 lemon
½ teaspoon maple syrup
1 slice grapefruit, to serve

Put ginger, lemongrass, turmeric and 1 cup water into a saucepan and simmer for 10 minutes. Strain and leave to cool. Top up with tonic, add lemon juice and maple syrup. Stir and serve cold with grapefruit slice.

Lemongrass, Ginger & Turmeric Tonic

Kombucha Tea

Snacks

You can be creative with a dipping sauce and elevate your dish to another level, whether it is as a base for a sandwich, a topping on a grain bowl to add extra flavor, or served with some crunchy vegetables or corn chips. Using cannellini beans and lentils, two superfood ingredients filled with prebiotics and fiber, you can easily make a dip or hummus, which is rich in flavor and packed with healthy protein.

BUTTERNUT & RED LENTIL HUMMUS

MAKES: 8 OZ
PREPARATION: 5 MINUTES
COOK: 20 MINUTES

2½ oz red lentils
3½ oz cooked butternut squash
½ teaspoon sea salt
1 teaspoon tahini
1 teaspoon chopped cilantro
2 tablespoons extra virgin olive oil
1 tablespoon lemon juice
salt and pepper

Put lentils into a saucepan, cover with water, bring to the boil then simmer for about 20 minutes, until soft. Drain and put them into a food processor with butternut squash, salt, tahini and cilantro and blitz for 1 minute. With machine still running, drizzle in oil and lemon juice and blend to a smooth consistency, adding some water, if needed. Season to taste.

RED PEPPER & HARISSA DIP

MAKES: 7 OZ
PREPARATION: 5 MINUTES
COOK: 0 MINUTES

3½ oz canned cannellini beans, drained and rinsed
2½ oz roasted red bell pepper
1 tablespoon extra virgin olive oil
1 teaspoon lemon juice
¼ teaspoon chopped cilantro
1 teaspoon harissa paste
½ garlic clove, chopped
salt and pepper

Put all ingredients into a food processor and pulse until smooth. Season with salt and pepper. Store in an airtight container in fridge for up to 7 days.

Butternut &
Red Lentil Hummus

Red Pepper &
Harissa Dip

Dressings

These two dressings are simple to make and are packed with superfood ingredients. Delicious and rich, both these dressings can be added to lots of dishes – use to top broiled, roasted or seared meat or simply toss them into a healthy soup.

SEEDY GREMOLATA

MAKES: 2¾ OZ
PREPARATION: 5 MINUTES
COOK: 0 MINUTES

1¾ oz mixed pumpkin and sunflower
   seeds, toasted and roughly
   chopped
grated zest of ½ lemon
1 tablespoon chopped parsley
¼ teaspoon chili flakes
1½ tablespoons extra virgin olive oil
salt and pepper

Mix seeds, lemon zest, parsley, chili and oil together in a bowl. Season with salt and pepper and serve. Store leftovers in an airtight container for 2 days.

MISO & WALNUT SAUCE

MAKES: 1 CUP
PREPARATION: 5 MINUTES
COOK: 10 MINUTES

5 Kalamata olives, pitted and
   roughly chopped
3½ fl oz extra virgin olive oil
2¾ oz red miso paste
1 garlic clove, grated
½ teaspoon chili flakes
1¾ oz walnuts, finely chopped

Put olives into a saucepan with oil over low heat. Add miso, garlic and chili and simmer for 5 minutes, stirring. Stir in walnuts and cook for another 2 minutes. Store in an airtight container in fridge for up to 3 days.

Miso & Walnut Sauce

Seedy Gremolata

Snacks

Deeply savory and fragrant with seeds, these crackers are a great afternoon snack served with a healthy dip while the delicious combination of oats, seeds and chocolate make these bars, packed with healthy protein and fats, an option all day long.

HIGH-FIBER DARK CHOCOLATE, OAT & SEED BARS

MAKES: 12
PREPARATION: 5 MINUTES
COOK: 20 MINUTES

1½ cups rolled (porridge) oats
3½ oz mixed seeds
¾ oz pistachios
⅓ cup maple syrup
1¾ oz dark chocolate chips
2 tablespoons coconut oil, melted

Preheat oven to 320°F. Lightly blitz oats in food processor, then put into a bowl and add rest of ingredients. Mix, then spread in a lined 8 inch square baking tin, pressing down well. Bake for 20 minutes or until golden brown. Cool, then cut into bars. Store in an airtight container for up to a week.

MIXED SEED CRACKERS

MAKES: 12 OZ
PREPARATION: 10 MINUTES
COOK: 20 MINUTES

7 oz mixed seeds (sunflower, pumpkin, chia, sesame, flax seeds)
1 teaspoon sea salt
1 tablespoon dried thyme
2 tablespoons extra virgin olive oil

Preheat oven to 320°F. Combine mixed seeds, salt and thyme in a large bowl. Add oil and 3½ fl oz water, mix together and leave for 10 minutes until seeds absorb the water. Put the dough onto a lined baking tray and cover with parchment paper. Using a rolling pin, spread dough out thinly, about ⅛–¼ inch. Remove paper and bake for 20 minutes, or until golden brown. Transfer to a wire rack to cool, then break into irregular shards and store in an airtight container for up to a week.

Mixed Seed
Crackers

High-fiber, Dark
Chocolate, Oat &
Seed Bars

28 days
Recipes

WITH

- A weekly shopping list for a whole month
- Menus for each day of the week for a month
- 3 recipes for each day of the week to help improve your gut health

Week 1

Fruit

- ○ 1 kiwi fruit
- ○ 1 banana
- ○ 2¾ oz raspberries or pitted cherries
- ○ 1 cup blueberries
- ○ 1 grapefruit
- ○ 3½ oz mixed fresh fruit
- ○ 1 cup strawberries
- ○ 5½ oz mixed melon
- ○ 1 oz grapes
- ○ 1 orange
- ○ 1¾ fl oz orange juice
- ○ 3 tbsp lime juice + 1 lime wedge
- ○ 2 tbsp lemon juice + 1 lemon wedge
- ○ 1 tsp grated lemon zest

Fridge Products

- ○ 5½ oz skin-on salmon fillet
- ○ 2 mackerel fillets
- ○ 2 skin-on, bone-in chicken thighs
- ○ 1¾ oz tempeh
- ○ 2 tbsp kimchi
- ○ 20 fl oz vegetable stock

Vegetables

- ○ 3½ red onions
- ○ 4 garlic cloves
- ○ 7 oz spinach
- ○ 5½ oz mixed mushrooms
- ○ 1½ fennel bulbs
- ○ ½ small winter cabbage
- ○ 5½ oz heirloom tomatoes
- ○ 2 tomatoes + 2 medium tomatoes
- ○ 5 cherry tomatoes
- ○ 1½ avocados
- ○ 1¾ oz baby arugula
- ○ 1¾ oz watercress
- ○ 2 oz cavolo nero (tuscan cabbage)
- ○ 8 small carrots
- ○ 2 zucchini, 1 yellow and 1 green
- ○ 1¾ oz soffritto (red onion, celery, carrot)
- ○ ¾ inch piece + 2 tsp grated fresh ginger
- ○ 2 tbsp cilantro
- ○ 2 tbsp parsley
- ○ 1 tsp chives
- ○ 2 tbsp basil
- ○ 1 rosemary sprig
- ○ 1 tsp mint
- ○ ¾ oz mixed herbs (basil, parsley, mint)
- ○ Handful kale leaves
- ○ Baby salad leaves (optional)

In the Storecupboard

- ○ 1 slice sourdough bread
- ○ 2¾ oz pappardelle pasta
- ○ 1¾ oz cooked brown rice
- ○ 4½ oz instant polenta
- ○ 10 oz green or brown lentils
- ○ 1¾ oz canned cranberry beans
- ○ 8½ oz canned garbanzo beans
- ○ 3½ oz canned cannellini beans
- ○ 13½ fl oz can coconut milk
- ○ 3½ oz spelt
- ○ 2 tbsp oats
- ○ 1½ oz granola
- ○ 1½ oz cashew nut butter
- ○ 3½ tbsp mixed toasted nuts
- ○ 1 tsp toasted pumpkin seeds
- ○ 10 pitted black olives
- ○ 1 tsp salted capers
- ○ rye flour
- ○ whole-wheat flour
- ○ baking powder
- ○ extra virgin olive oil
- ○ balsamic vinegar
- ○ maple syrup
- ○ honey
- ○ harissa paste
- ○ garam masala
- ○ poppy seeds
- ○ ground turmeric
- ○ paprika

- ○ chili flakes
- ○ saffron threads

Eggs & Dairy Products

- ○ 3½ fl oz kefir milk
- ○ 1 tbsp whole milk
- ○ ¾ cup live yogurt
- ○ 7 oz Greek yogurt
- ○ 3½ oz labneh
- ○ 1¾ oz Taleggio cheese
- ○ 1 oz parmesan
- ○ 2¾ oz feta
- ○ 3½ oz ricotta
- ○ 2 oz butter
- ○ 5 large eggs

Monday

A delicious and super healthy way to start the week, the kefir smoothie loaded with probiotics and superfoods, is naturally sweet and made without added sugars.

Breakfast

BALANCE KEFIR SMOOTHIE

SERVES: 1
PREPARATION: 5 MINUTES
COOK: 0 MINUTES

1 kiwi fruit
1 banana
2¾ oz raspberries or pitted cherries
2 tablespoons oats
3½ fl oz kefir milk
1¾ fl oz orange juice

Peel and slice kiwi fruit and banana. Put into a blender with remaining ingredients and blend until smooth. Serve immediately.

Lunch

TURMERIC & COCONUT DAL

SERVES: 4
PREPARATION: 5 MINUTES
COOK: 30 MINUTES

2 tablespoons extra virgin olive oil
1 red onion, finely diced
¾ inch piece ginger, peeled and grated
1 teaspoon ground turmeric
2 teaspoons garam masala
7 oz brown or green lentils
13½ fl oz can coconut milk
1¾ oz spinach, chopped
1 tablespoon chopped cilantro
salt and pepper
Greek yogurt, to serve

Heat oil in a large saucepan over medium heat and cook onion and ginger for 3 minutes, or until softened. Stir in spices and, after 2 minutes, add lentils, 13½ fl oz boiling water and coconut milk. Bring to the boil, then simmer over low heat for 25 minutes. Add spinach and stir. Season to taste, sprinkle with cilantro and serve with Greek yogurt. Store rest of dal in fridge for another day or freeze for later.

Dinner

CREAMY MUSHROOM & TALEGGIO POLENTA

SERVES: 1 + ENOUGH FOR CHUNKY POLENTA (PAGE 54)
PREPARATION: 5 MINUTES
COOK: 12 MINUTES

2 tablespoons extra virgin olive oil
1 garlic clove, thinly sliced
1 red onion, sliced
5½ oz mixed mushrooms, sliced
1 tablespoon chopped parsley
4½ oz instant polenta
1 oz butter
1¾ oz Taleggio cheese, sliced
salt and pepper

Heat oil in a frying pan over medium heat and fry garlic and onion for 1 minute. Add mushrooms and cook for 5 minutes. Remove from heat and add parsley. Meanwhile, bring 2 cups water to the boil in a large saucepan. Pour in polenta, stirring constantly for 5 minutes, or until it leaves side of pan but it is still runny. Remove from heat, add butter and season to taste. Divide mixture in half. Spread one half on a tray and store in fridge for another day. Top other half with Taleggio slices and grill until melting. Add mushrooms and serve immediately.

Balance Kefir Smoothie

Turmeric & Coconut Dal

*Creamy Mushroom
& Taleggio Polenta*

Tuesday

Cabbage not only has impressive health benefits, but is also cost effective and tastes delicious when caramelized and paired with the protein-rich lentils.

Breakfast

DIY GRANOLA WITH YOGURT & FRUIT

SERVES: 1
PREPARATION: 2 MINUTES
COOK: 0 MINUTES

3½ oz live yogurt (page 28)
1½ oz granola (page 34)
3½ oz mixed fresh fruit, sliced

Spoon half of yogurt into base of a bowl. Add half quantity of granola and fruit. Repeat layers.

Lunch

FENNEL, GRAPEFRUIT & POPPY SEED SALAD WITH SALMON

SERVES: 1
PREPARATION: 5 MINUTES
COOK: 15 MINUTES

5½ oz salmon fillet, skin on
1 oz live yogurt (page 28)
1 tablespoon extra virgin olive oil
½ teaspoon poppy seeds
1 grapefruit, cut into segments
½ fennel bulb, thinly sliced
1 teaspoon chopped chives
salt and pepper

Preheat oven to 375°F. Lay salmon, skin-side down, on a baking tray, season with salt and pepper and bake for 15 minutes, or until cooked. Cool, then flake into large chunks and set aside. Meanwhile, mix yogurt, oil and poppy seeds together in a small bowl, then season with salt and pepper. Mix grapefruit with fennel and half the dressing, toss and arrange on a plate. Arrange salmon on top, drizzle with remaining dressing and sprinkle with chives.

Dinner

CARAMELIZED ROAST CABBAGE WITH LENTILS

SERVES: 1
PREPARATION: 5 MINUTES
COOK: 35 MINUTES

4 tablespoons extra virgin olive oil
½ small red onion, chopped
2¾ oz brown or green lentils
1¾ oz tomatoes, chopped
1 tablespoon balsamic vinegar
2 teaspoons honey
½ small winter cabbage, halved
1 teaspoon chopped parsley
salt and pepper

Heat 1 tablespoon oil in a large saucepan over medium heat and cook onion for 3 minutes, or until softened. Add lentils, tomatoes and 5 fl oz hot water, bring to the boil, then simmer for 30 minutes. Season to taste. Meanwhile, combine 2 tablespoons oil, the vinegar and honey in a small bowl. Brush cabbage wedges with dressing and season with salt and pepper. Heat remaining oil in a frying pan and cook cabbage on both sides for 15 minutes, or until edges are golden brown, brushing frequently with dressing. Spoon lentils onto a plate, add cabbage wedges and sprinkle with parsley.

DIY Granola with
Yogurt & Fruit

Fennel, Grapefruit & Poppy
Seed Salad with Salmon

Caramelized Roast
Cabbage with Lentils

Wednesday

A day full of fermented foods, adding depth to your diet and the health benefits that come from live microbes, which thrive in foods such as kimchi, tempeh and yogurt.

Breakfast

SMASHED EGG ON SOURDOUGH TOAST WITH KIMCHI

SERVES: 1
PREPARATION: 1 MINUTE
COOK: 3 MINUTES

2 large eggs
1 tablespoon whole milk
¼ oz butter
1 slice sourdough bread, toasted
2 tablespoons kimchi
salt and pepper

Whisk eggs and milk together in a small bowl, then season with salt and pepper. Heat a small frying pan for 1 minute, then add butter and let it melt. Pour in eggs and leave for 20 seconds, then stir with a wooden spoon, mixing and folding until eggs are softly set. Arrange on toast and add kimchi.

Lunch

CHUNKY POLENTA & AVOCADO SALAD WITH TEMPEH

SERVES: 1
PREPARATION: 5 MINUTES
COOK: 10 MINUTES

½ quantity polenta (from Monday)
3 tablespoons extra virgin olive oil
1¾ oz tempeh, cut into cubes
1 small avocado, thinly sliced
1¾ oz baby arugula
1¾ oz watercress
1 tablespoon balsamic vinegar
salt

Remove polenta from fridge and put it onto a clean surface. Using a sharp knife, cut into ¾ x 4 inch batons. Heat 1 tablespoon oil in a non-stick frying pan over medium heat and cook batons for 5 minutes, or until crisp and golden. Set aside. In same pan, heat 1 tablespoon oil, add tempeh and cook for 5 minutes, or until brown on both sides. Put avocado, arugula and watercress in a bowl, season with salt, remaining oil and vinegar, then arrange on a plate and top with polenta and tempeh. Serve.

Dinner

GARBANZO BEAN & SAFFRON SOUP WITH LIVE YOGURT

SERVES: 2
PREPARATION: 5 MINUTES
COOK: 10 MINUTES

1 tablespoon extra virgin olive oil
1 small red onion, finely chopped
8½ oz canned garbanzo beans, drained and rinsed
10 fl oz vegetable stock
pinch of saffron threads
1¾ oz live yogurt (page 28)
1 teaspoon paprika (optional)
1 tablespoon cilantro

Heat oil in a large saucepan over medium heat and cook onion for 3 minutes, or until softened. Stir in garbanzo beans and stock, bring to a simmer and cook for a few minutes. Purée 2¾ oz of garbanzo beans with 7–8½ fl oz stock, then put into a bowl and whisk in saffron and yogurt. Add a few tablespoons of broth to loosen up mixture if necessary. Whisk mixture back into soup, stirring and cooking for another 5 minutes. Ladle into a bowl and sprinkle with paprika, if liked, and cilantro. Store rest of soup in fridge for another day.

Smashed Egg on Sourdough Toast with Kimchi

Chunky Polenta & Avocado Salad with Tempeh

Garbanzo Bean & Saffron Soup with Live Yogurt

Thursday

Cashew butter is full of monounsaturated fatty acids, healthy protein and vitamins, but try to opt for an unsweetened unsalted variety when buying.

Breakfast

STRAWBERRIES & 'CASHEW' CREAM

SERVES: 1
PREPARATION: 5 MINUTES
COOK: 0 MINUTES

1½ oz cashew nut butter
½ oz honey
pinch of salt
1 cup strawberries, quartered
1 teaspoon chopped toasted nuts

Stir cashew butter, honey and salt together, adding a few tablespoons water until sauce becomes a thick consistency. Put into a serving bowl, arrange strawberries on top, then sprinkle with toasted nuts.

Lunch

HEIRLOOM TOMATO, BEAN & FETA SALAD

SERVES: 1
PREPARATION: 5 MINUTES
COOK: 0 MINUTES

5½ oz heirloom tomatoes, sliced
1¾ oz canned cranberry beans,
   drained and rinsed
1 tablespoon extra virgin olive oil
1¾ oz feta, crumbled
1 tablespoon basil leaves
salt and pepper

Arrange tomatoes on a plate and season with salt. In a small bowl, season beans with a drizzle of oil, salt and pepper. Arrange beans over tomatoes, then scatter over feta and basil.

Dinner

PAPPARDELLE WITH CAVOLO NERO & PARMESAN

SERVES: 1
PREPARATION: 5 MINUTES
COOK: 10 MINUTES

2¾ oz pappardelle pasta
2 oz cavolo nero (tuscan cabbage),
   tough ribs removed
2 tablespoons extra virgin olive oil
1 garlic clove, chopped
¼ teaspoon chili flakes
1 oz parmesan, grated
1 tablespoon mixed toasted nuts
salt and pepper

Bring 4 cups water to the boil in a large saucepan. Add salt and cook pasta according to packet instructions until al dente. Meanwhile, chop cavolo nero roughly and blanch it in another saucepan of boiling water for 5 minutes. Drain well. Heat oil in a frying pan and fry garlic and chili flakes for 1 minute. Add cavolo nero, season well and cook for another 2 minutes. Drain pasta, reserving 1 tablespoon cooking water. Add pasta to frying pan and mix together thoroughly with parmesan and reserved cooking water for 1 minute. Sprinkle with toasted nuts.

Strawberries & 'Cashew' Cream

Heirloom Tomato, Bean & Feta Salad

Pappardelle with Cavolo Nero & Parmesan

Friday

Roasted harissa carrots is a recipe that should be made when carrots are fresh and young at the peak of the season. This recipe is easy to make and can be used as a side dish to many other dishes.

Breakfast

MIXED MELON & AVOCADO SALAD WITH GINGER-HONEY DRESSING

SERVES: 1
PREPARATION: 5 MINUTES
COOK: 0 MINUTES

2 teaspoons grated ginger
1½ oz honey
2 tablespoons lime juice
3 tablespoons extra virgin olive oil
5½ oz mixed melon, cut into 1 inch wedges
½ avocado, cut into 1 inch wedges
1 oz grapes, cut lengthways
salt and pepper

Pulse ginger, honey and lime juice in a food processor to combine. While processor is running, slowly add oil to emulsify dressing. Season to taste. Put melon, avocado and grapes into a bowl, drizzle with dressing and toss to coat.

Lunch

ROASTED HARISSA CARROTS WITH LIVE LABNEH

SERVES: 1
PREPARATION: 5 MINUTES
COOK: 30 MINUTES

1 tablespoon harissa paste, plus extra to serve
1 tablespoon maple syrup
1 tablespoon extra virgin olive oil
1 teaspoon lemon juice
8 small carrots
3½ oz labneh
2 tablespoons mixed toasted nuts
salt

Preheat oven to 375°F. In a small bowl, mix harissa, maple syrup, oil and lemon juice together, then season with salt. Set aside. Peel carrots, leaving 2 inches of green top. Add carrots to a baking dish and drizzle with harissa sauce. Toss to coat and add 2 tablespoons water. Roast carrots for 30 minutes, or until soft, adding a splash of water if getting dry. Serve carrots with labneh and sprinkled with toasted nuts on top and a dash of harissa.

Dinner

PAN-ROASTED CHICKEN WITH ORANGE & OLIVES

SERVES: 1
PREPARATION: 40 MINUTES
COOK: 25 MINUTES

1 orange
2 skin-on, bone-in chicken thighs
1 garlic clove, sliced
1 rosemary sprig
1 tablespoon extra virgin olive oil
10 black olives, pitted
large handful of kale
1 teaspoon chopped parsley
salt and pepper

Grate zest of orange, squeeze half and cut rest into slices. Set aside. In a bowl, marinate chicken thighs with orange zest and juice, garlic, rosemary and salt and pepper for 30 minutes. Heat oil in an ovenproof frying pan over medium-high heat, add chicken and cook for 3 minutes on each side. Add orange slices, olives and kale and mix thoroughly for a few minutes. Roast in oven for 15–20 minutes until chicken is cooked through. Sprinkle with parsley and serve.

Mixed Melon & Avocado Salad
with Ginger-Honey dressing

Roasted Harissa Carrots
with Live Labneh

Pan-roasted Chicken
with Orange & Olives

Saturday

A great way to add vegetables to your plate, zucchini noodles can be the star of so many dishes from pasta-style bowls to salads to stir-fries.

Breakfast

HERBY SPINACH SHAKSHUKA

SERVES: 1
PREPARATION: 5 MINUTES
COOK: 15 MINUTES

1 tablespoon extra virgin olive oil
½ garlic clove, crushed
¾ oz mixed herbs (basil, parsley, mint)
3½ oz spinach, roughly chopped
1 teaspoon ground turmeric
1 tablespoon lime juice
2 eggs
salt and pepper
sourdough bread (toasted) and lime wedge, to serve

Heat oil in a frying pan over medium heat and fry garlic for 1 minute, then add herbs and cook, stirring for about 5 minutes. Add spinach and mix to incorporate herbs. Add turmeric and season with salt and pepper. Add 1¾ fl oz water and cook until nearly evaporated, then add lime juice and mix. Make 2 small wells in spinach and crack an egg into each. Cover with a lid and cook for 3–5 minutes until eggs are set, then serve with toast and lime wedge.

Lunch

STUFFED TOMATOES

SERVES: 1
PREPARATION: 5 MINUTES
COOK: 10 MINUTES

2 tomatoes
1¾ oz cooked brown rice
1 oz feta, crumbled
1 teaspoon chopped mint
1 teaspoon chopped parsley
1 tablespoon extra virgin olive oil
pepper
baby salad leaves, to serve (optional)

Preheat oven to 350°F. Cut tops off tomatoes and remove flesh. Discard seeds, chop flesh and set aside with tops. Season tomatoes and put, cut-side down, on a baking tray. In a small bowl, mix tomato flesh with rice, feta and herbs and season with pepper. Divide mixture between tomatoes, drizzle with oil, cover with tomato tops and bake for 10 minutes. Serve with salad leaves, if desired.

Dinner

ZUCCHINI NOODLES WITH RICOTTA & BASIL

SERVES: 1
PREPARATION: 5 MINUTES
COOK: 2 MINUTES

2 zucchini, 1 yellow and 1 green
1 tablespoon extra virgin olive oil
½ garlic clove, sliced
3½ oz ricotta
1 teaspoon grated lemon zest
1 tablespoon lemon juice
1 tablespoon chopped basil
1 teaspoon toasted pumpkin seeds

Using a julienne peeler, cut zucchini into thin noodles. Heat oil in a non-stick frying pan over medium heat and fry garlic for 1 minute. Add zucchini noodles and toss to coat. Remove from heat and arrange them on a plate. Top with ricotta, lemon zest and juice, and basil. Sprinkle with pumpkin seeds and serve.

Herby Spinach Shakshuka

Stuffed Tomatoes

Zucchini Noodles
with Ricotta & Basil

Sunday

The left-over pancakes from breakfast and the stew from dinner can be stored in the fridge for up to two days. Instead of spelt in the stew, use wheat berries.

Breakfast

RYE PANCAKES WITH BLUEBERRIES & GREEK YOGURT

SERVES: 2 / MAKES: 4
PREPARATION: 5 MINUTES
COOK: 10 MINUTES

3 oz rye flour
3 oz whole-wheat flour
2 teaspoons baking powder
1 large egg, lightly whisked
3 tablespoons maple syrup
5½ oz Greek yogurt
½ oz butter
1 cup blueberries
salt

Whisk flours, baking powder and a pinch of salt together in a bowl. In another bowl, mix egg with 1 tablespoon maple syrup and 3½ oz yogurt. Add to dry ingredients and mix until just combined. Heat a frying pan over medium heat, add half the butter and let it melt. Ladle 1¾ oz batter into pan, sprinkle with some blueberries and cook for 2 minutes. When bottom has set, flip using a palette knife and cook for another 1 minute. Repeat until all batter is used. Serve with remaining blueberries, yogurt and syrup.

Lunch

PAN-ROASTED MACKEREL WITH FENNEL & CAPERS

SERVES: 1
PREPARATION: 10 MINUTES
COOK: 15 MINUTES

1 teaspoon salted capers
1 tablespoon extra virgin olive oil
1 small fennel bulb, cut into wedges
2 mackerel fillets or fish of choice
juice of ½ lemon
salt and pepper
lemon wedge, to serve

Soak capers for 5 minutes, then rinse and repeat twice more. Drain. Heat oil in a non-stick frying pan over medium heat and cook fennel for 3 minutes. Add capers and cook for another 2 minutes, then set aside. Season fish with salt and pepper, add to pan and cook for 3 minutes each side. Add fennel mixture and lemon juice and cook for another 2 minutes. Serve with lemon wedge.

Dinner

SPELT & BEAN STEW

SERVES: 2
PREPARATION: 5 MINUTES
COOK: 40 MINUTES

2 tablespoons extra virgin olive oil, plus extra for drizzling
1¾ oz soffritto (chopped red onion, celery, carrot)
5 cherry tomatoes, halved
3½ oz spelt
10 fl oz vegetable stock
1¾ oz spinach, roughly chopped
3½ oz canned cannellini beans, drained and rinsed

Heat oil in a large saucepan over medium heat and cook soffritto and tomatoes for 3 minutes. Add spelt and cook for another 3 minutes, stirring constantly. Add stock, bring to the boil, then simmer for 30 minutes, or until spelt is tender. Stir spinach and beans into soup and cook for another 5 minutes until spinach wilts. Drizzle with oil. Store rest of stew in fridge for another day.

Rye Pancakes with
Blueberries & Greek Yogurt

Pan-roasted Mackerel
with Fennel & Capers

Spelt &
Bean Stew

Vegetables

- ⃝ 5½ oz butternut squash
- ⃝ 10½ oz purple potatoes
- ⃝ 3½ oz mixed mushrooms + 1 large flat mushroom
- ⃝ ¾ oz arugula
- ⃝ 2 oz watercress
- ⃝ 1 large tomato + 2 tomatoes
- ⃝ 1¾ oz green beans
- ⃝ 2 yellow zucchini
- ⃝ 1 green zucchini
- ⃝ 1 round purple or big black eggplant
- ⃝ 1 lb 5 oz cherry tomatoes
- ⃝ 4 oz ripe tomatoes
- ⃝ 2¾ oz broccoli
- ⃝ 1 oz kale leaves
- ⃝ 1 small cucumber
- ⃝ 1 lb 2 oz cauliflower
- ⃝ 1¾ oz yellow bell pepper
- ⃝ 1 avocado
- ⃝ 1¾ small red onions
- ⃝ 1 French shallot
- ⃝ 2½ garlic cloves
- ⃝ 1 tsp grated fresh ginger
- ⃝ 4 tbsp soffritto (onion, carrot, celery)
- ⃝ 3 scallions
- ⃝ 2½ tbsp parsley
- ⃝ 2¾ oz basil leaves
- ⃝ 2½ tbsp mint leaves
- ⃝ ½ lemongrass stalk
- ⃝ 1½ tsp oregano
- ⃝ ¾ oz mixed sprouts

Fruit

- ⃝ 2 bananas
- ⃝ ½ apple
- ⃝ 2 dried apricots
- ⃝ ½ cup blueberries
- ⃝ 1 tbsp berries
- ⃝ 3½ fl oz organic apple juice
- ⃝ 1¾ oz mixed fresh fruit
- ⃝ 1 pink grapefruit
- ⃝ 1 orange
- ⃝ 2 tbsp lime juice
- ⃝ 4 tbsp lemon juice + grated zest 1 lemon + lemon wedge
- ⃝ 1 peach
- ⃝ 1 oz pomegranate seeds

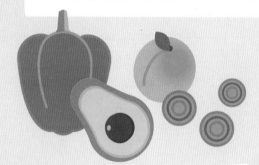

Fridge Products

- ⃝ 5½ oz beef rump steak
- ⃝ 2 lamb chops
- ⃝ 3½ oz frozen mixed seafood
- ⃝ 2 mackerel fillets
- ⃝ 33 fl oz vegetable stock
- ⃝ 1 tbsp pickles + 2¼ oz pickled radish

In the Storecupboard

- ○ 4 slices sourdough bread + 1¾ oz sourdough bread
- ○ 2¾ oz paella rice
- ○ 9 oz canned cannellini beans
- ○ 7 oz canned plum tomatoes
- ○ 7 oz canned chopped tomatoes
- ○ 1¾ oz garbanzo beans
- ○ 1¾ oz millet
- ○ 2¾ oz pearl barley
- ○ 1¾ oz freekeh
- ○ ¾ oz rolled (porridge) oats
- ○ ¾ oz barley flakes
- ○ ¾ oz rye flakes
- ○ 4½ oz almond flour
- ○ 1½ oz oat flour
- ○ 2 oz all-purpose flour
- ○ 3 oz whole-wheat flour
- ○ 4½ oz besan (chickpea flour)
- ○ 1¾ oz whole-wheat couscous
- ○ 1 tablespoon white wine
- ○ 4 fl oz maple syrup
- ○ 1¾ oz triple nut butter
- ○ 1 tbsp toasted mixed nuts
- ○ 2½ tbsp pine nuts
- ○ extra virgin olive oil
- ○ balsamic vinegar
- ○ white wine vinegar
- ○ ground turmeric
- ○ chili flakes
- ○ sumac
- ○ saffron
- ○ ground cinnamon
- ○ baking powder and baking soda

- ○ harissa spice
- ○ honey

Eggs & Dairy Products

- ○ 2 tbsp butter
- ○ 3½ oz halloumi
- ○ 2¼ oz parmesan
- ○ 2 tbsp cream
- ○ 1¾ oz mozzarella
- ○ 5½ oz burrata
- ○ 1¾ oz feta
- ○ 1⅓ cups kefir milk
- ○ 2 tbsp Greek yogurt
- ○ 5 oz live yogurt
- ○ 4 eggs + 1 egg yolk

Monday

Wholegrain freekeh contains more fiber and protein than standard wheat and it is a source of calcium, potassium, iron and zinc. It is a good addition to soups and salads.

Breakfast

TRIPLE NUT BUTTER TOAST WITH BANANA

SERVES: 1
PREPARATION: 5 MINUTES
COOK: 2 MINUTES

1 slice sourdough bread
1¾ oz triple nut butter (page 32)
1 banana, sliced

Toast bread, spread with nut butter and arrange banana slices over.

Lunch

ROAST SQUASH, HALLOUMI & FREEKEH WARM SALAD

SERVES: 1
PREPARATION: 5 MINUTES
COOK: 25 MINUTES

5½ oz butternut squash, peeled and cut into ¾–1¼ inch chunks
2 tablespoons extra virgin olive oil
1 teaspoon harissa spice
1¾ oz freekeh
1¾ oz halloumi, sliced
1 tablespoon lemon juice
1 oz pomegranate seeds
salt and pepper

Preheat oven to 350°F. Put squash into a roasting pan, toss with oil, harissa and season to taste. Roast for 20 minutes, or until squash is golden and softened, turning them over after 10 minutes. Meanwhile bring 13½ fl oz water to the boil in a medium saucepan. Add freekeh and simmer for 20 minutes, or until tender. Stir freekeh into roasting pan and roast for another 2 minutes. Heat a frying pan over high heat and fry halloumi for 1–2 minutes on each side until golden. Transfer squash and freekeh mix to a plate, add lemon juice and mix. Arrange halloumi on top and sprinkle over pomegranate seeds.

Dinner

GNOCCHI WITH MUSHROOM RAGOUT

SERVES: 2
PREPARATION: 5 MINUTES
COOK: 30 MINUTES

10½ oz purple potatoes, peeled and halved
2 oz all-purpose flour
1 egg yolk, whisked
1 tablespoon extra virgin olive oil
½ garlic clove, chopped
3½ oz mixed mushrooms, sliced
1 tablespoon grated parmesan
1 teaspoon chopped parsley
salt

Boil potatoes in a saucepan of water until tender. Drain, cool and mash in a bowl. Add flour, salt and egg yolk and mix well. Transfer to a lightly floured work surface and knead to a dough. Divide dough into pieces and roll each piece into a long sausage, ¾ inch in diameter. Cut sausage into ½–¾ inch chunks, then press down gently on each chunk with a fork. Leave on a plate, spaced apart. Heat oil in a frying pan and fry garlic and mushrooms for 5 minutes. Bring 2 cups salted water to the boil and cook gnocchi until they float on surface. Using a slotted spoon, transfer them to frying pan and fry for 2 minutes with parmesan and parsley. Serve. Store rest in fridge for another day.

Triple Nut Butter Toast
with Banana

Roast Squash, Halloumi
& Freekeh Warm Salad

Gnocchi with
Mushroom Ragout

Tuesday

Created to get people to eat more fruit, Bircher muesli is great for a quick breakfast, simple and delicious with the smoothness of the oats and the crunchiness of the apple. You can use an unpeeled pear instead.

Breakfast

BIRCHER MUESLI

SERVES: 1
PREPARATION: 5 MINUTES
SOAK: OVERNIGHT

½ apple, unpeeled and coarsely grated
¾ oz rolled (porridge) oats
¾ oz barley flakes
¾ oz rye flakes
2 dried apricots, chopped
3½ fl oz organic apple juice
1 tablespoon berries
1 tablespoon chopped toasted nuts

Put apple, oats, barley and rye flakes, apricots and apple juice into a bowl and stir well. Cover bowl and leave to soak overnight in fridge. Next morning, stir muesli, then top with berries and nuts.

Lunch

CHARGRILLED STEAK & PICKLE OPEN SANDWICH

SERVES: 1
PREPARATION: 5 MINUTES
COOK: 10 MINUTES

5½ oz beef rump steak
1 large flat mushroom
2 tablespoons extra virgin olive oil
1 large slice sourdough bread
¾ oz arugula
1 tablespoon pickled radish (page 36)
1 tablespoon pickles
salt and pepper

Preheat a chargrill pan over medium heat. Drizzle steak and mushroom with 1 tablespoon oil, season and cook for 4 minutes on each side until cooked to your preference. Let steak rest 5 minutes before slicing. Brush bread with remaining oil and cook in pan for 30 seconds on each side. Top with mushroom, arugula, steak, radish and pickles.

Dinner

PROVENÇAL PISTOU SOUP

SERVES: 2
PREPARATION: 5 MINUTES
COOK: 25 MINUTES

⅓ cup extra virgin olive oil
2 tablespoons soffritto (finely chopped onion, carrot, celery)
1 large tomato, peeled and chopped
1¾ oz green beans, sliced into 2 inch pieces
1 yellow zucchini, diced
7 oz canned cannellini beans, drained and rinsed
½ garlic clove
1¾ oz basil leaves
¾ oz parmesan, grated
salt and pepper

Heat 2 tablespoons oil in a large saucepan over medium heat and cook soffritto for 3 minutes. Add tomato, cook for a few minutes, then stir in green beans and zucchini and cook for 5 minutes, stirring. Add cannellini beans and 1 cup water or just enough to cover vegetables. Bring to the boil, then simmer for 10 minutes. Meanwhile, add garlic, basil, parmesan, pinch of salt and remaining oil to a blender and blend until basil is finely chopped. Season soup to taste, ladle into a bowl and top with a dollop of pistou. Store both in fridge for another day.

Bircher Muesli

Chargrilled Steak &
Pickle Open Sandwich

Provençal
Pistou Soup

Wednesday

A source of fiber and low in fat and sugar, eggplants are full of vitamins and minerals. Broiling them will make this classic bake even healthier.

Breakfast

ONE-POT EGG WITH SCALLION

SERVES: 1
PREPARATION: 5 MINUTES
COOK: 12 MINUTES

2 tablespoons cream
1 teaspoon chopped parsley
¼ teaspoon chili flakes
2 scallions, roughly chopped
1 egg
¼ teaspoon sumac
salt and pepper
1 slice sourdough bread, toasted

Preheat oven to 340°F. Butter a ramekin dish and add 1 tablespoon cream, then add parsley, chili flakes and half the scallion. Make an indent in mix and crack in egg. Add the remaining cream, season with salt and pepper and put ramekin into a small roasting pan half-filled with hot water. Bake for 12 minutes, then sprinkle remaining scallion and sumac on top. Serve with toast.

Lunch

EGGPLANT PARMIGIANA

SERVES: 2
PREPARATION: 20 MINUTES
COOK: 1 HOUR

1 large eggplant, cut into ¼ inch slices
1 tablespoon extra virgin olive oil
½ small red onion, chopped
7 oz canned plum tomatoes, mashed
½ oz basil leaves
1¾ oz mozzarella, drained and sliced
1 tablespoon grated parmesan
salt

Put eggplant into a colander and sprinkle salt between layers. Put a plate on top, then a weight over plate and leave in sink for 15 minutes. Preheat oven to 350°F. Heat oil in a large saucepan over medium heat and cook onion for 3 minutes. Add tomatoes, splash of water and 2 basil leaves. Season with salt and cook for 15 minutes. Rinse eggplant and pat dry. Heat a griddle pan and broil eggplant for 8 minutes on both sides. Spread a spoonful of tomato sauce in a small ovenproof dish and alternate with layers of eggplant, sauce, mozzarella, parmesan and basil until all ingredients are used. Bake in oven for 25 minutes. Rest 30 minutes, then serve. Store rest in fridge for another day.

Dinner

SEAFOOD PAELLA

SERVES: 1
PREPARATION: 5 MINUTES
COOK: 25 MINUTES

½ tablespoon extra virgin olive oil
¼ small red onion, chopped
2¾ oz paella rice
1 tablespoon white wine
3½ oz can chopped tomatoes
7½ fl oz vegetable stock
½ large pinch of saffron
3½ oz frozen mixed seafood, thawed and sliced
½ tablespoon chopped parsley
salt and pepper

Heat oil in a large frying pan over medium heat and fry onion for 3 minutes. Add rice and stir for 1 minute, splash in wine and once evaporated, add tomatoes, stock and saffron. Season and cook for 15 minutes, stirring occasionally. Add seafood, mix and simmer for 5 minutes, then sprinkle over parsley and serve immediately.

One-pot Egg
with Scallion

Eggplant
Parmigiana

Seafood Paella

Thursday

Even if the live probiotic culture will die when the kefir is heated, being 99 per cent lactose-free makes it a good substitute for those who are lactose intolerant. It will also make these pancakes extra fluffy.

Breakfast

ALMOND & KEFIR PANCAKES WITH FRUIT & YOGURT

SERVES: 2 / MAKES: 4
PREPARATION: 5 MINUTES
COOK: 10 MINUTES

1 large egg, separated
2½ oz almond flour
1½ oz oat flour
1 teaspoon baking powder
½ teaspoon ground cinnamon
4½ fl oz kefir milk
butter, for frying
2 tablespoons Greek yogurt
1¾ oz mixed fresh fruit

Whisk egg white in a bowl. Whisk egg yolk, flours, baking powder, cinnamon and kefir in another bowl until smooth, then fold in egg white. Heat a frying pan over medium heat, add a dollop of butter and let it melt, then pour in 2 tablespoons of batter and cook for 2–3 minutes on each side, flipping over with a spatula. Repeat until all the batter is used. Serve with yogurt and fruit. Store rest in fridge for another day.

Lunch

BALSAMIC ZUCCHINI, FETA & PINE NUT SALAD

SERVES: 1
PREPARATION: 5 MINUTES
COOK: 0 MINUTES

1 tablespoon balsamic vinegar
1 tablespoon extra virgin olive oil
1 tablespoon lemon juice
1 zucchini, cut lengthways into ¼ inch slices
1 yellow zucchini, cut lengthways into ¼ inch slices
1 tablespoon mint leaves
1 tablespoon pine nuts, toasted
1¾ oz feta, crumbled
salt and pepper

Put vinegar into a small bowl and season with salt and pepper. Gradually whisk in oil and lemon juice. Put zucchini into a large bowl with mint and drizzle over dressing. Toss gently to combine, then sprinkle over feta and pine nuts and serve.

Dinner

BARLEY, CANNELLINI, TOMATO & WATERCRESS STEW

SERVES: 2
PREPARATION: 5 MINUTES
COOK: 35 MINUTES

2¾ oz pearl barley
2 tablespoons extra virgin olive oil
1 French shallot, sliced
½ teaspoon chili flakes
1 cup vegetable stock
1¾ oz canned cannellini beans, drained and rinsed
2 tomatoes, chopped
2 oz watercress
1 tablespoon grated parmesan
salt and pepper

Put barley into a medium saucepan, cover with water and cook for 20 minutes. Drain and set aside. Heat 1 tablespoon oil in another pan over medium heat and cook shallot and chili flakes for 2 minutes. Add stock, simmer for 5 minutes, then add barley, beans and tomatoes and cook for 10 minutes. Season to taste. Blitz 1 oz watercress with remaining oil and the parmesan in a food processor until smooth. Ladle stew into a bowl, swirl in watercress salsa and top with remaining watercress. Store rest in fridge for another day.

Almond & Kefir Pancakes
with Fruit & Yogurt

Balsamic Zucchini, Feta
& Pine Nut Salad

Barley,
Cannellini, Tomato
& Watercress Stew

Friday

Kale, a very popular leafy green from the cruciferous family, is rich in nutrients. Freeze the rest of the soup for later, then defrost before reheating until piping hot.

Breakfast

CITRUS SALAD WITH LEMONGRASS, GINGER & TOASTED NUTS

SERVES: 1
PREPARATION: 5 MINUTES
COOK: 0 MINUTES

1 tablespoon lime juice
1 teaspoon grated fresh ginger
½ lemongrass stalk, thinly sliced
1 tablespoon honey
1 pink grapefruit
1 orange, peeled and sliced
   crossways
1 teaspoon pine nuts, toasted
1 teaspoon mint leaves

Combine lime juice, ginger, lemongrass and honey in a small bowl and set aside. Using a small knife, peel and remove white pith from grapefruit, then cut in between membrane to release segments. Arrange fruits on a plate, drizzle over juice mixture and sprinkle with pine nuts and mint.

Lunch

CHARRED-ROASTED BROCCOLI & HALLOUMI MILLET PILAF

SERVES: 1
PREPARATION: 5 MINUTES
COOK: 20 MINUTES

2¾ oz broccoli, cut into small florets
1¾ oz halloumi, sliced
2 tablespoons extra virgin olive oil
½ teaspoon chili powder
½ teaspoon oregano
1¾ oz millet
¾ oz mixed sprouts
1 tablespoon lime juice
salt and pepper

Preheat oven to 400°F. Put broccoli and halloumi into a roasting pan. Drizzle with 1 tablespoon oil, add chili and oregano, season with salt and pepper, then toss well. Bake for 15–20 minutes. Toast millet in a medium saucepan for 2 minutes. Very carefully add 3½ fl oz water, a pinch of salt and stir. Bring to the boil, then simmer for 15 minutes. Leave off heat for 10 minutes, then fluff with a fork. Put millet, broccoli, halloumi and sprouts onto a platter and mix together, adding remaining oil, the lime juice and salt if needed.

Dinner

ROAST TOMATO & CRISPY KALE SOUP

SERVES: 2
PREPARATION: 5 MINUTES
COOK: 50 MINUTES

1 lb 5 oz cherry tomatoes
3 tablespoons extra virgin olive oil
2 tablespoons soffritto (finely
   chopped onion, carrot, celery)
1¾ oz canned garbanzo beans,
   drained and rinsed
1 cup vegetable stock
1 oz kale leaves, stems removed
   and leaves cut into small pieces
1 tablespoon live yogurt (page 28)
salt and pepper

Preheat oven to 400°F. Put tomatoes into a roasting tray and toss with 1 tablespoon oil. Season with salt and roast for 35 minutes. Reduce oven temperature to 320°F. Heat 1 tablespoon oil in a saucepan over medium heat and cook soffritto for 5 minutes. Add tomatoes, garbanzo beans and stock, then blitz with a stick blender until smooth. Coat kale with remaining oil, season, spread out over a baking tray and bake for 10 minutes, or until crisp, tossing after 5 minutes. Ladle soup into a bowl, swirl in a spoonful of yogurt and sprinkle with crispy kale.

Citrus Salad with
Lemongrass, Ginger
& Toasted Nuts

Charred-roasted
Broccoli & Halloumi
Millet Pilaf

Roast Tomato &
Crispy Kale Soup

Saturday

Store the remaining muffins for breakfast either in an airtight container in the fridge for two days or freeze them for another time. If there is too much cauliflower purée for dinner then store in the fridge for up to three days.

Breakfast

BANANA & BLUEBERRY KEFIR MUFFINS

MAKES: 6
PREPARATION: 5 MINUTES
COOK: 25 MINUTES

3 oz whole-wheat flour
2 oz almond flour
1 teaspoon baking powder
1 teaspoon baking soda
pinch of salt
1 tablespoon extra virgin olive oil
1 ripe banana, mashed
4 fl oz maple syrup
7 fl oz kefir milk
½ cup blueberries

Preheat oven to 350°F. Line a 6-hole muffin tin with paper cases. Mix flours, baking powder, baking soda and salt together. In another bowl, mix oil, banana, maple syrup and kefir. Combine both mixtures and mix gently to just combine. Add half quantity of blueberries and mix again. Divide batter into muffin cases, top each muffin with 2 blueberries. Bake for 25 minutes, or until golden brown.

Lunch

PANZANELLA SALAD WITH TOMATOES, BURRATA & PEACH

SERVES: 1
PREPARATION: 5 MINUTES
COOK: 5 MINUTES

4 oz ripe tomatoes, chopped into bite-sized pieces
1 tablespoon extra virgin olive oil, plus extra for drizzling
1¾ oz sourdough bread, cut into cubes
1 peach, thinly sliced
1 tablespoon basil leaves
1 small cucumber, thinly sliced
5½ oz burrata, torn
salt

Put tomatoes into a bowl and season with salt. Set aside. Heat 1 tablespoon oil in a frying pan, add bread cubes and toast, tossing until golden brown. Transfer tomatoes and bread to a serving bowl, add peach, basil and cucumber. Drizzle with oil and add burrata.

Dinner

MEDITERRANEAN MACKEREL WITH CAULIFLOWER PURÉE

SERVES: 1
PREPARATION: 5 MINUTES
COOK: 25 MINUTES

1 lb 2 oz cauliflower, chopped
4½ oz live yogurt (page 28)
1 cup vegetable stock
1 tablespoon butter
½ garlic clove, grated
1 teaspoon white wine vinegar
1 teaspoon oregano
1 tablespoon extra virgin olive oil, plus extra to drizzle
2 mackerel fillets
salt and pepper
lemon wedge, to serve

Bring cauliflower, yogurt and stock to the boil in a large saucepan, then simmer for 20 minutes. Drain cauliflower and reserve 2 tablespoons of cooking liquid. Blitz cauliflower and butter in a food processor, and, if necessary, the reserved liquid, until smooth. Combine garlic, vinegar, oregano and oil in a small bowl. Season. Drizzle fillets with oil and season. Cook, skin-side down first, in a frying pan for 2 minutes on each side. Put purée onto a plate, top with fish and drizzle over dressing. Serve with lemon wedge.

*Banana & Blueberry
Kefir Muffins*

*Panzanella Salad with
Tomatoes, Burrata & Peach*

*Mediterranean Mackerel
with Cauliflower Purée*

Sunday

Any remaining garbanzo bean pancakes for lunch can be wrapped up and kept in the fridge for up to three days. Just reheat them in a pan until they are warm throughout.

Breakfast

BAKED EGGS WITH TOMATOES & BELL PEPPER

SERVES: 1
PREPARATION: 5 MINUTES
COOK: 10 MINUTES

1 tablespoon extra virgin olive oil
½ small red onion, thinly sliced
3½ oz canned chopped tomatoes
1¾ oz yellow bell pepper, sliced
2 eggs
½ teaspoon chili flakes
1 slice sourdough bread, toasted

Heat oil in a large frying pan over medium heat and fry onion for 3 minutes. Add tomatoes, pepper and 1¾ fl oz water, bring to the boil, then simmer for 5 minutes. Make 2 indents and crack in eggs, then cover and cook over low heat until eggs are ready. Sprinkle with chili flakes and serve on toast.

Lunch

GARBANZO BEAN PANCAKES WITH AVOCADO & PICKLES

SERVES: 1
PREPARATION: 5 MINUTES
COOK: 10 MINUTES

1 teaspoon live yogurt (page 28)
1 teaspoon lemon juice
1 avocado, roughly mashed
2 tablespoons extra virgin olive oil
1 scallion, finely chopped
¼ teaspoon ground turmeric
1 teaspoon chopped parsley
4½ oz besan (chickpea flour)
1 teaspoon baking powder
salt and pepper
1¾ oz pickled radish (page 36), to serve

Combine yogurt, lemon juice and avocado in a bowl. Season. Heat 1 tablespoon oil in a frying pan and fry scallion, turmeric and parsley for 3 minutes. Season and set aside. Whisk flour and baking powder together in a large bowl, then while whisking, slowly add 5 fl oz water to a smooth, thick but not quite pourable batter. Mix in scallion mixture. Whisk until smooth. Heat a frying pan over medium heat and add remaining oil. Add a quarter of the batter and cook for 2 minutes on each side. Remove and keep pancake warm. Repeat with remaining batter. Serve with avocado mix and pickled radish.

Dinner

MARINATED LAMB CHOPS WITH COUSCOUS SALAD

SERVES: 1
PREPARATION: 40 MINUTES
COOK: 20 MINUTES

1¾ oz whole-wheat couscous
1 tablespoon each chopped mint and parsley
1 tablespoon pine nuts, toasted
grated zest and juice of 1 lemon
1 garlic clove, very finely chopped
4 tablespoons extra virgin olive oil
2 lamb chops

Cook couscous according to packet instructions, then put it into a bowl with herbs, pine nuts, half of lemon zest and juice. Set aside. Combine remaining lemon zest and juice, the garlic and oil and use to coat lamb chops on both sides. Cover and rest in fridge for 30 minutes. Heat broiler to high and broil lamb chops for 5 minutes on each side, or until internal temperature is 130°F. Cover with foil and rest for 5 minutes before serving with couscous.

*Baked Eggs with Tomatoes
& Bell Pepper*

*Garbanzo Bean Pancakes
with Avocado & Pickles*

*Marinated Lamb Chops
with Couscous Salad*

Fruit

- ○ 1 lb 3 oz fresh raspberries
- ○ 1 tbsp mixed berries
- ○ 1¾ oz fresh or dried blueberries
- ○ 2 bananas
- ○ 1 tbsp pomegranate seeds
- ○ 2 tbsp lemon juice + 2 lemons

Eggs & Dairy Products

- ○ 1 small mozzarella ball
- ○ 1 oz parmesan
- ○ 2¾ oz goat cheese
- ○ 3½ oz feta
- ○ 1¾ oz labneh
- ○ 1½ oz butter
- ○ 9 oz live yogurt
- ○ 5½ oz Greek yogurt
- ○ 15 fl oz kefir milk
- ○ 5 eggs + 1 egg white

Vegetables

- ○ 5½ oz spinach
- ○ 1 small cauliflower
- ○ 1 sweet potato + 1 ordinary potato
- ○ 5½ oz purple potatoes
- ○ 2 purple eggplants
- ○ 3½ oz chestnut or button mushrooms
- ○ 2 red bell peppers
- ○ 2 zucchini + 2½ oz zucchini
- ○ 2 yellow zucchini
- ○ 3½ oz mixed salad leaves (arugula, spinach)
- ○ handful of arugula
- ○ handful of salad cress
- ○ baby salad leaves
- ○ 5½ oz cavolo nero (tuscan cabbage)
- ○ 5½ oz cabbage
- ○ 5½ oz Swiss chard
- ○ 6 asparagus spears
- ○ 1 avocado
- ○ 1 tomato
- ○ 6 garlic cloves
- ○ 2 scallions
- ○ 1 small red onion
- ○ 3 tbsp soffritto (red onion, carrot, celery)
- ○ 1 small carrot
- ○ 1 bouquet garni of parsley, thyme, sage
- ○ 4 tbsp parsley
- ○ ½ oz basil leaves
- ○ 1 tbsp dill
- ○ 1 small bunch of thyme

In the Storecupboard

- ○ 3 rye bread slices
- ○ 1 sourdough bread slice + 5½ oz stale sourdough
- ○ 2 whole-wheat tortillas
- ○ 3½ oz green or brown lentils
- ○ 3 oz spelt + spelt or barley to serve
- ○ 3½ oz quinoa
- ○ 5½ oz whole-wheat couscous
- ○ ½ cup rolled (porridge) oats + 1 tsp blitzed oats
- ○ 10 oz granola
- ○ 7 oz canned cannellini beans
- ○ 1 oz Kalamata olives
- ○ 1 oz walnuts
- ○ ¼ oz pine nuts
- ○ 1 tbsp mixed nuts
- ○ 2 tsp mixed seeds
- ○ 4 tbsp chia seeds
- ○ whole-wheat buckwheat flour
- ○ oat flour
- ○ extra virgin olive oil
- ○ rapeseed oil
- ○ maple syrup
- ○ honey
- ○ superfine sugar
- ○ red wine & white wine vinegar
- ○ balsamic vinegar
- ○ sumac
- ○ paprika
- ○ mixed spice
- ○ acai powder
- ○ baking powder

Fridge & Freezer Products

- ○ 1¾ oz frozen edamame beans
- ○ 3½ oz frozen mixed berries
- ○ 5½ oz salmon fillet
- ○ 2½ oz smoked salmon
- ○ 5½ oz flank steak
- ○ 4 skin-on chicken thighs
- ○ 1¾ oz tempeh
- ○ 20 fl oz vegetable stock
- ○ 2 tbsp pickled cucumber
- ○ 2 oz kimchi
- ○ 1 tbsp miso paste
- ○ 1¾ oz silken tofu

Monday

The chia jam is not only great on toast, but it can be swirled through porridge or in yogurt. This recipe works well with any juicy fruits like berries or peaches, apricots and cherries.

Breakfast

CHIA JAM ON RYE TOAST

SERVES: 1
PREPARATION: 5 MINUTES
COOK: 5 MINUTES

1 lb 2 oz fresh raspberries
1 tablespoon lemon juice
4 tablespoons honey
4 tablespoons chia seeds
1 large slice rye bread

Cook fruit in a small saucepan over medium heat for 5 minutes, or until it breaks down. Remove from heat, mash fruit with back of a spatula, then add lemon juice and honey. Stir in chia seeds and mix to combine. Leave to set for about 5 minutes. Toast rye bread and spread with a dollop of chia jam.

Lunch

MOZZARELLA & ZUCCHINI SALAD WITH PESTO

SERVES: 1
PREPARATION: 5 MINUTES
COOK: 0 MINUTES

½ garlic clove
pinch of salt
½ oz basil leaves
¼ oz pine nuts
½ oz parmesan, grated
¾ fl oz extra virgin olive oil
1 each green and yellow zucchini, thinly sliced
1 small mozzarella ball, torn

For pesto, put garlic and salt into a mortar and start crushing until creamy consistency. Add basil and crush leaves by rotating pestle until a green liquid comes out. Add pine nuts and parmesan and reduce to a cream. To make pesto creamier, while stirring with pestle, add oil in a steady stream until combined. Put zucchini and mozzarella onto a plate, drizzle over pesto sauce and toss to combine. Serve.

Dinner

BAKED SWEET POTATO WITH WHIPPED FETA & SUMAC

SERVES: 1
PREPARATION: 5 MINUTES
COOK: 1 HOUR

1 sweet potato
1¾ oz feta, crumbled
1½ oz live yogurt (page 28)
½ teaspoon sumac
1 teaspoon extra virgin olive oil
salt and pepper
1 tablespoon kimchi (page 26)

Preheat oven to 430°F. Prick sweet potato all over with a fork and bake for 1 hour, or until golden on outside and soft inside. In a small bowl, cream together feta and yogurt and season with salt and pepper. Top potato with whipped feta, sprinkle with sumac, drizzle over oil and add kimchi. Serve.

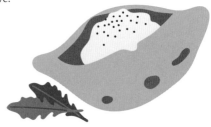

Chia Jam on
Rye Toast

Mozzarella & Zucchini
Salad with Pesto

Baked Sweet Potato with
Whipped Feta & Sumac

Tuesday

A traditional Breton dish, this savory pancake is a perfect healthy lunch burst with antioxidants and fiber from the buckwheat and vitamins and protein from the spinach.

Breakfast

LIVE YOGURT PARFAIT

SERVES: 1
PREPARATION: 5 MINUTES
COOK: 0 MINUTES

5½ oz live yogurt (page 28)
1 teaspoon honey
2 tablespoons chia jam (page 82)
2 tablespoons granola (page 34)

Mix yogurt and honey together in a bowl. In a small jar, alternate layers of yogurt and jam, finishing with granola.

Lunch

SPINACH & GOAT CHEESE BUCKWHEAT GALETTE

SERVES: 1
PREPARATION: 5 MINUTES
COOK: 15 MINUTES

2 tablespoons extra virgin olive oil
1 garlic clove, chopped
1¾ oz spinach, chopped
1 oz goat cheese, crumbled
2¾ oz whole-wheat buckwheat flour
1 egg, whisked
10 fl oz kefir milk
1½ oz butter
salt and pepper

Heat 1 tablespoon oil in a frying pan over medium heat and fry garlic for 2 minutes. Add spinach and stir for 3 minutes. Remove from heat, season and fold in cheese. Set aside. Beat flour, egg, half the kefir and a pinch of salt together in a bowl to a smooth paste, then add remaining kefir to loosen mixture. Melt butter and stir into batter. Lightly oil a frying pan with ½ tablespoon oil and heat over medium–high heat. Spoon in half of the batter and cook for 3 minutes. Spread over half of filling, leaving a ¾ inch border, then fold over edges leaving center exposed and cook for 2 minutes. Remove and repeat with remaining batter. Serve.

Dinner

GRILLED EGGPLANT & LENTIL SALAD

SERVES: 1
PREPARATION: 5 MINUTES
COOK: 30 MINUTES

1 purple eggplant, thickly sliced
2 tablespoons extra virgin olive oil
1 garlic clove, very finely chopped
1 tablespoon soffritto (finely chopped red onion, carrot, celery)
3½ oz green or brown lentils
1¾ oz mixed salad (arugula, spinach)
salt and pepper

Preheat oven to 350°F. Place eggplant on a baking tray, drizzle with ½ tablespoon oil, garlic and a pinch of salt and bake for 25 minutes. Heat 1 tablespoon oil in a saucepan over medium heat and cook soffritto for 3 minutes. Add lentils, cover with water and cook for 25 minutes, or until all water has evaporated. Transfer lentils to a plate, add salad, remaining ½ tablespoon oil, season to taste and mix. Scatter over eggplant and mix slightly. Serve.

Live Yogurt
Parfait

Spinach & Goat Cheese
Buckwheat Galette

Grilled Eggplant
& Lentil Salad

Wednesday

This classic Italian soup for lunch elevates beans and vegetables to another level, Ribollita, in Italian 'twice-boiled', means that the next day the soup is even tastier.

Breakfast

ACAI BOWL

SERVES: 1
PREPARATION: 5 MINUTES
COOK: 0 MINUTES

⅓ cup kefir milk
5½ oz Greek yogurt
3½ oz frozen mixed berries
1 banana, sliced
1½ tablespoons acai powder
1 tablespoon mixed nuts, toasted
1 tablespoon mixed fresh berries
1 teaspoon mixed seeds

In a blender, put kefir, yogurt, frozen berries, banana and acai powder and blend until smooth and creamy. Transfer to a bowl and top with nuts, fresh berries and seeds.

Lunch

RIBOLLITA

SERVES: 4
PREPARATION: 5 MINUTES
COOK: 45 MINUTES

2 tablespoons extra virgin olive oil
2 tablespoons soffritto (finely
   chopped carrot, celery, red onion)
1 potato, diced
5½ oz cavolo nero (tuscan cabbage),
   tough stems removed and leaves
   chopped
5½ oz cabbage, tough stems removed
   and leaves chopped
5½ oz Swiss chard, chopped
7 oz canned cannellini beans,
   drained and rinsed
5½ oz stale sourdough bread,
   roughly chopped
salt and pepper

Heat oil in a pan over medium heat and fry soffritto for 3 minutes. Add potato, cook for 2 minutes, then add cavolo nero, cabbage, Swiss chard and 4 cups boiling water. In a blender, blend half of cannellini beans with 1 cup hot water, then pour into pan. Bring to the boil and cook for 30 minutes, stirring occasionally. Add remaining beans and bread, season with salt and pepper and cook for another 10 minutes until bread has softened and absorbed some of the liquid. Serve. Store leftovers in fridge for another time.

Dinner

SALMON FISHCAKES & PICKLE

SERVES: 1
PREPARATION: 35 MINUTES
COOK: 15 MINUTES

1 bouquet garni of parsley, thyme,
   sage
½ lemon, sliced
1 garlic clove, sliced
5½ oz salmon fillet
5½ oz purple potatoes, peeled
   and cut into ¾ inch cubes
1 tablespoon oat flour
2 tablespoons extra virgin olive oil
salt and pepper
2 tablespoons pickled cucumber
   (page 36), baby salad leaves and
   lemon wedge, to serve

Combine bouquet garni, sliced lemon, garlic, a pinch of salt and 5 fl oz water in a large saucepan and bring to the boil. Add salmon and cook for 5 minutes. Remove from liquid, cool slightly, then flake salmon into a bowl. Cook potatoes in another pan of salted boiling water, drain, then mash with a fork. Add to salmon, together with flour and some of the herbs of the bouquet garni. Season and divide mixture into 3 fishcakes. Cover and rest in fridge for 30 minutes. Heat oil in a large frying pan and cook fishcakes for 3 minutes on each side. Serve with pickled cucumber, salad and lemon wedge.

Acai Bowl

Ribollita

*Salmon Fishcakes
& Pickle*

Thursday

This dinner is economical, healthy and scrumptious. Plus it is really quick to make if you have left-over cooked barley, brown rice or quinoa from the night before..

Breakfast

BLUEBERRY GRANOLA COOKIES

MAKES: 12
PREPARATION: 5 MINUTES
COOK: 20 MINUTES

9 oz granola (page 34)
1¾ oz fresh or dried blueberries
1 egg white
1 tablespoon superfine sugar

Preheat oven to 340°F. Combine granola and blueberries in a bowl. In another bowl, beat egg white with an electric mixer until foamy. Add sugar and beat until soft peaks form. Fold in granola mixture until evenly coated. Using damp hands, divide mixture into 12 balls, then flatten each with palms of hands. Put them onto a lined baking tray and bake for about 20 minutes, rotating baking tray halfway through, until golden brown. Store in an airtight container for up to 5 days.

Lunch

ASPARAGUS & POACHED EGG

SERVES: 1
PREPARATION: 5 MINUTES
COOK: 10 MINUTES

1 large slice sourdough bread
6 asparagus spears
1 teaspoon extra virgin olive oil
1 teaspoon white wine vinegar
1 egg
salt and pepper

Heat a griddle pan over high heat, toast bread and set aside. Chargrill asparagus for 2 minutes on each side, drizzle with oil, season with salt and pepper and arrange on bread. Bring a saucepan of salted water to the boil, add vinegar and reduce heat to simmer. Crack egg into a small bowl, create a whirlpool in simmering water with a spoon and pour egg into center. Cook for 2–3 minutes, then remove with a slotted spoon and put on top of asparagus. Sprinkle with pepper and serve.

Dinner

STUFFED PEPPERS WITH SPELT & GOAT CHEESE

SERVES: 1
PREPARATION: 5 MINUTES
COOK: 25 MINUTES

2 tablespoons extra virgin olive oil
3½ oz chestnut or button mushrooms, sliced
3 oz cooked spelt
1¾ oz goat cheese, crumbled
1 teaspoon chopped parsley
1 red bell pepper, halved lengthways and seeded
1 teaspoon blitzed rolled oat crumbs
salt and pepper
arugula, to serve

Preheat oven to 350°F. Heat 1 tablespoon oil in a large frying pan and cook mushrooms for 5 minutes. Season with salt and pepper and place together with spelt in a bowl. Add cheese and parsley and stir to combine. Arrange bell pepper halves, cut-side up, on a baking tray and season with a pinch of salt. Divide mixture evenly between peppers, sprinkle with oat crumbs and bake for 20 minutes until bell peppers are soft and oats are golden. Serve with arugula.

Blueberry Granola Cookies

Asparagus &
Poached Egg

Stuffed Peppers with
Spelt & Goat Cheese

Friday

Easy to make, in less than 10 minutes, this lunch is filled with plant-based proteins and fiber. You can cook the quinoa ahead of time and freeze until ready to use.

Breakfast

SUPER GREEN FRITTERS

SERVES: 1 / MAKES: 4
PREPARATION: 15 MINUTES
COOK: 6 MINUTES

2½ oz zucchini, grated
2 oz spinach, chopped
2 small eggs
1 tablespoon roughly chopped dill
1 tablespoon parmesan, grated
2 tablespoons oat flour
2 tablespoons rapeseed oil
1¾ oz labneh
½ garlic clove, very finely chopped
salt and pepper
lemon wedge, to serve

Combine zucchini, spinach, eggs, dill and parmesan in a bowl. Season with salt and pepper, add flour and mix again. Rest for 10 minutes. Heat oil in a non-stick frying pan over medium heat. Using a large serving spoon, divide mixture into four equal portions and cook for 3 minutes on each side. Make dip by mixing labneh and garlic together in a bowl. Season to taste. Serve fritters with dip and lemon wedge.

Lunch

QUINOA SALAD WITH TEMPEH & CANDIED WALNUTS

SERVES: 1
PREPARATION: 5 MINUTES
COOK: 7 MINUTES

1 teaspoon butter
1 tablespoon superfine sugar
1 oz walnuts
1 teaspoon balsamic vinegar
1½ tablespoons extra virgin olive oil
1 teaspoon honey
3½ oz cooked quinoa
1¾ oz tempeh, diced
1¾ oz salad leaves of choice
salt

Melt butter and sugar in a frying pan, add walnuts and stir until completely coated. Arrange on a lined baking tray, separating them with a fork, then sprinkle with a pinch of salt and set aside. For dressing, mix vinegar, ½ tablespoon oil, honey and a pinch of salt together in a small bowl. Set aside. Heat remaining 1 tablespoon oil in a frying pan and cook tempeh, stirring, for 5 minutes, or until lightly browned. Mix all ingredients together in a bowl, drizzle with dressing and toss to combine.

Dinner

BEEF TACOS WITH KIMCHI SAUCE

SERVES: 1
PREPARATION: 35 MINUTES
COOK: 6 MINUTES

1 teaspoon balsamic vinegar
1 small red onion, very finely chopped
1 tablespoon extra virgin olive oil
½ teaspoon paprika
2 teaspoons chopped parsley
5½ oz flank steak
1 tomato, diced
1 oz kimchi, chopped (page 26)
2 whole-wheat tortillas
small handful of spinach leaves

Combine vinegar, ½ onion, oil, paprika and 1 teaspoon parsley in a large, wide bowl, add steak, coat evenly, cover and rest in fridge for 30 minutes. For kimchi sauce, combine tomato, remaining onion, kimchi and remaining parsley in another bowl. Set aside. Preheat a griddle pan over medium heat and cook steak for 3 minutes on each side. Remove from pan, cover and rest for 5 minutes. Warm tortillas, cut steak into strips, put into tortilla and top with kimchi sauce and spinach. Serve.

Super Green Fritters

Quinoa Salad with Tempeh & Candied Walnuts

Beef Tacos with Kimchi Sauce

Saturday

This creamy cauliflower soup for dinner can be made ahead of time and stored in the freezer. You can swap the cauliflower for the green and purple varieties, as well as the sweeter Romanesco cauliflower.

Breakfast

OAT BANANA PANCAKES WITH RASPBERRIES

SERVES: 1 / MAKES: 4
PREPARATION: 5 MINUTES
COOK: 5 MINUTES

2¼ fl oz kefir milk
1 egg, separated
1 small banana, roughly chopped
1 teaspoon baking powder
1 tablespoon maple syrup, plus extra
  to serve
½ cup rolled (porridge) oats
1 teaspoon rapeseed oil
2 tablespoons raspberries

Mix kefir, egg yolk, banana, baking powder, maple syrup and oats in a blender. In a bowl, whisk egg white until frothy, then gently fold in the oat mixture. Heat oil in a non-stick frying pan over medium heat, add 2 tablespoons of batter and cook for 1–2 minutes on each side. Repeat with remaining batter. Serve with syrup and raspberries.

Lunch

GRIDDLED VEGETABLES & FETA COUSCOUS

SERVES: 2
PREPARATION: 5 MINUTES
COOK: 20 MINUTES

1 each small green and yellow
  zucchini, sliced
1 small eggplant, sliced
1 red bell pepper, sliced
5½ oz whole-wheat couscous
2 tablespoons chopped parsley
2 tablespoons extra virgin olive oil
1¾ oz feta, crumbled
1 tablespoon pomegranate seeds
salt and pepper

Heat a griddle pan over high heat and chargrill vegetables for 5–8 minutes until tender. Put couscous into a large bowl with 5 fl oz boiling water, cover and leave for 10–12 minutes until water is absorbed. Using a fork, fluff up couscous, add vegetables, parsley and oil. Season to taste and mix well. Spoon onto a plate and add feta and pomegranate seeds. Serve. Store leftovers in fridge for another time.

Dinner

CAULIFLOWER SOUP

SERVES: 1
PREPARATION: 5 MINUTES
COOK: 15 MINUTES

1 tablespoon extra virgin olive oil
1 garlic clove, sliced
1 teaspoon mixed spice
1 small cauliflower, cut into florets
10 fl oz vegetable stock
1 teaspoon chopped parsley
1 teaspoon toasted seeds
salt and pepper

Heat oil in a large saucepan over medium heat and cook garlic and spice for 1 minute. Add cauliflower and stir for 1 minute before adding stock. Bring to the boil, then simmer for 10 minutes, or until cauliflower is tender. Transfer to blender and blitz until creamy and smooth. Pour soup back into pan, season with salt and pepper and simmer for 2 minutes. Ladle into a bowl and sprinkle with parsley and seeds.

Oat Banana Pancakes
with Raspberries

Griddled Vegetables
& Feta Couscous

Cauliflower Soup

Sunday

A favorite option for many, this breakfast has the additional benefit of plant-based protein, fiber and other essential nutrients from the edamame beans.

Breakfast

AVOCADO & EDAMAME TOAST WITH SMOKED SALMON

SERVES: 1
PREPARATION: 5 MINUTES
COOK: 5 MINUTES

1¾ oz frozen edamame beans, thawed
1 avocado
2 tablespoons live yogurt (page 28)
1 tablespoon lemon juice
2 slices rye bread, toasted
2½ oz smoked salmon
handful of salad cress
salt and pepper
lemon wedge, to serve

Steam edamame beans for 5 minutes, then blitz half in a blender with 2 tablespoons water. Scoop avocado flesh into a bowl, add blended edamame, yogurt and lemon juice and mix with a fork. Fold in remaining edamame, season with salt and pepper and divide between toasted bread. Add smoked salmon, sprinkle over some pepper and top with cress. Serve with lemon wedge.

Lunch

ONE-POT MISO SOUP

SERVES: 1
PREPARATION: 5 MINUTES
COOK: 12 MINUTES

10 fl oz vegetable stock
1 garlic clove, sliced
2 scallions, sliced
1 small carrot, julienned
1¾ oz silken tofu, diced
1 tablespoon miso paste

Bring stock to the boil in a large saucepan. Add garlic, scallions and carrot, cover with a lid and simmer for 5 minutes. Add tofu and simmer for 3 minutes, then turn off heat. In a small bowl, loosen up miso paste with 1 tablespoon stock, then pour it into pan. Serve.

Dinner

PAN-ROASTED CHICKEN WITH OLIVES, LEMON & THYME

SERVES: 2
PREPARATION: 35 MINUTES
COOK: 30 MINUTES

4 skin-on chicken thighs
3 tablespoons red wine vinegar
2 tablespoons extra virgin olive oil
1 oz Kalamata olives, pitted
1 small lemon, sliced
1 small bunch of thyme
salt and pepper
1 portion cooked spelt or pearl barley, to serve

Put chicken into a shallow dish, add vinegar and oil, cover and marinate in fridge for 30 minutes. Heat a frying pan over high heat and sear chicken thighs, skin-side down, for 5 minutes. Turn over and cook for about 10 minutes. Add olives, lemon and thyme, cook for 10–15 minutes until chicken is cooked. Season and serve with spelt. Store leftovers in fridge for later.

Avocado & Edamame
Toast with Smoked Salmon

One-pot Miso Soup

Pan-roasted Chicken with
Olives, Lemon & Thyme

Fruit

- ○ 4½ bananas
- ○ 1¼ oz mixed berries
- ○ 2 Medjool dates
- ○ 1 pear
- ○ ½ apple
- ○ ⅓ cup blueberries + extra to serve
- ○ kiwi fruit to serve
- ○ 1 oz pomegranate seeds
- ○ ½ lime
- ○ 2 lemons + lemon wedge

Eggs & Dairy Products

- ○ 17 fl oz kefir milk
- ○ 1 cup milk of your choice
- ○ 2 oz live yogurt
- ○ 6 oz Greek yogurt
- ○ ½ oz parmesan
- ○ 1½ tbsp butter
- ○ 1¾ oz feta
- ○ 3½ oz halloumi cheese
- ○ 1 oz Taleggio cheese
- ○ 6 eggs

Vegetables

- ○ 5 cherry tomatoes
- ○ 9 oz ripe tomatoes + extra to garnish
- ○ 5½ oz small beets
- ○ 2 red bell peppers
- ○ 1 small cucumber
- ○ handful of arugula
- ○ 3½ oz mixed salad leaves
- ○ 3½ oz Jerusalem artichokes
- ○ ½ small radicchio
- ○ 14 oz sweet potatoes
- ○ 7 oz rainbow chard
- ○ 3 kale leaves
- ○ 5 small red onions
- ○ 3 garlic cloves
- ○ 1 scallion
- ○ 2½ tbsp parsley
- ○ 1 bouquet garni with thyme, rosemary, sage, bay leaves
- ○ 1 tbsp mint
- ○ 1 tsp chives
- ○ 3 thyme sprigs
- ○ 1½ tbsp cilantro

In the Storecupboard

- ○ 1 large slice rye bread
- ○ 2 slices sourdough bread
- ○ 2¾ oz sourdough bread for crostini
- ○ 2½ oz buckwheat noodles
- ○ 6¼ oz rolled (porridge) oats
- ○ 3½ oz canned cranberry beans
- ○ 9 oz mixed dried beans
- ○ 5¼ oz canned garbanzo beans
- ○ 3½ oz canned brown or green lentils
- ○ 5½ oz dried fava beans
- ○ 3½ fl oz canned coconut milk
- ○ 2¾ oz quinoa
- ○ 1 oz bulgur wheat
- ○ 2¾ oz spelt
- ○ 2¾ oz freekeh
- ○ ½ oz whole almonds
- ○ 1 tsp toasted mixed nuts
- ○ 2½ tbsp chia seeds
- ○ 1 tbsp hazelnuts
- ○ 7 oz mixed seeds
- ○ ½ tbsp sesame seeds
- ○ 1¾ oz almond flour
- ○ ⅓ cup whole-wheat flour
- ○ 10½ oz spelt flour
- ○ ¾ oz cornstarch
- ○ extra virgin olive oil
- ○ rapeseed oil
- ○ 2½ fl oz coconut oil
- ○ ½ oz green olives
- ○ ¼ oz salted capers
- ○ Dijon mustard
- ○ 1 tbsp white wine

- ○ apple cider vinegar
- ○ red wine vinegar
- ○ balsamic vinegar
- ○ honey
- ○ maple syrup
- ○ superfine sugar
- ○ mirin
- ○ chili sauce
- ○ dark chocolate chips
- ○ soy sauce
- ○ baking powder
- ○ chili flakes
- ○ ground turmeric
- ○ ground cinnamon
- ○ curry powder
- ○ spirulina powder

Fridge & Freezer Products

- ○ 7 oz skinless, boneless chicken breast
- ○ 5½ oz tuna steak
- ○ 1 salmon fillet
- ○ 2¾ oz firm tofu
- ○ 2¾ oz silken tofu
- ○ 5 cups vegetable stock
- ○ 2 tbsp pickles
- ○ 5½ oz frozen mixed berries

Monday

Beets are part of the same family as spinach and, being low in fat, full of antioxidants, vitamins and minerals, they can be called health-food giants.

Breakfast

SPICY SCRAMBLED EGGS ON RYE TOAST

SERVES: 1
PREPARATION: 5 MINUTES
COOK: 8 MINUTES

2 eggs
½ teaspoon ground turmeric
1 large slice rye bread
1 teaspoon butter
5 cherry tomatoes, halved
½ teaspoon chili flakes
1 tablespoon chopped cilantro

In a small bowl, mix eggs and turmeric together. Heat a small frying pan over low heat, toast bread and set aside. In same pan, add butter, tomatoes and chili and cook for 3 minutes. Add eggs and cook, stirring, for 2–3 minutes. Serve eggs on toasted bread sprinkled with cilantro leaves.

Lunch

SLOW-COOKED BEETS WITH FETA

SERVES: 1
PREPARATION: 5 MINUTES
COOK: 1 HOUR

5½ oz small beets, halved
1 small red onion, cut into wedges
¼ teaspoon chili flakes
1 tablespoon red wine vinegar
1 tablespoon extra virgin olive oil
1¾ oz feta, sliced
salt and pepper

Preheat oven to 350°F. Scrunch and wet 2 pieces of parchment paper. Put beets, onion, chili and vinegar into a roasting pan lined with 1 piece wet baking paper, drizzle with oil, season with salt and pepper and cover with other piece of paper. Bake for 1 hour, or until tender. Remove top paper and sprinkle over feta.

Dinner

SPICY FAJITA BUDDHA BOWL WITH BEANS

SERVES: 1
PREPARATION: 5 MINUTES
COOK: 10 MINUTES

1 tablespoon extra virgin olive oil
1 small red bell pepper, sliced
1 small red onion, sliced
1¾ oz canned cranberry beans, drained and rinsed
¼ teaspoon chili flakes
¼ cup quinoa, cooked
½ tablespoon chopped cilantro
juice of ½ lime
1¾ oz mixed salad leaves, chopped
salt and pepper

Heat oil in a medium saucepan over medium heat and cook red bell pepper and onion for 5 minutes. Season and add beans and chili with 1 tablespoon water. Mix well and cook for another 5 minutes. Mix quinoa, cilantro and lime juice together in a bowl. Put salad leaves in a serving bowl, then top with quinoa, red pepper and bean mixture and serve.

NEVER GIVE UP

*Spicy Scrambled Eggs
on Rye Toast*

*Slow-cooked Beets
with Feta*

*Spicy Fajita Buddha
Bowl with Beans*

Tuesday

Onions are full of antioxidants and the pairing with the protein, fiber and mineral content of the sweet potatoes, makes this dinner unbeatable.

Breakfast

KEFIR, BANANA & BERRIES SMOOTHIE

SERVES: 1
PREPARATION: 5 MINUTES
COOK: 0 MINUTES

5 fl oz kefir milk
½ banana, sliced
1¼ oz mixed berries
½ oz whole almonds, toasted
2 Medjool dates, pitted and chopped

Put all ingredients into a blender and blitz until smooth. Serve.

Lunch

JERUSALEM ARTICHOKE & POACHED CHICKEN SALAD

SERVES: 1
PREPARATION: 5 MINUTES
COOK: 30 MINUTES

3½ oz Jerusalem artichokes,
   cut into chunks
4 tablespoons extra virgin olive oil
1 pear, cut in half lengthways,
   then into 6 wedges, stalks
   and core removed
3½ oz skinless, boneless chicken
   breast
1 thyme sprig
½ lemon, sliced
1 teaspoon balsamic vinegar
1 tablespoon honey
salt and pepper

Preheat oven to 400°F. Put artichokes into a roasting pan, toss with 1 tablespoon oil, season and roast for 25 minutes. Add pear and roast for another 5 minutes. Put chicken, thyme and lemon into a large saucepan, cover with cold water, bring to the boil, then simmer for 10 minutes, or until cooked. Drain well and when cool enough, shred chicken into pieces. Set aside. For dressing, whisk remaining 3 tablespoons oil, vinegar and honey together in a bowl. Season. Drizzle dressing over artichokes, toss and add chicken.

Dinner

SWEET POTATO & RED ONION SOUP

SERVES: 2
PREPARATION: 5 MINUTES
COOK: 20 MINUTES

1 tablespoon extra virgin olive oil
1 small red onion, sliced
14 oz sweet potatoes, peeled
   and diced
13½ fl oz vegetable stock
1 teaspoon toasted mixed nuts
1 teaspoon chopped chives
1 tablespoon Greek yogurt
salt and pepper
sourdough bread, to serve

Heat oil in a large saucepan over medium heat and cook onion for 3 minutes. Add sweet potatoes, cook for 2 minutes, then add stock and simmer for 15 minutes. Blend soup with a stick blender and season to taste. Ladle soup into a bowl, sprinkle over nuts, chives and add dollop of yogurt. Serve with bread. Store leftovers in fridge for another time.

Kefir, Banana & Berries Smoothie

Jerusalem Artichoke & Poached Chicken Salad

Sweet Potato & Red Onion Soup

Wednesday

Overnight oats can be stored in the fridge for up to five days, which makes this an ideal breakfast meal prep to make on Sunday night to enjoy during the week.

Breakfast

EASY OVERNIGHT OATS

SERVES: 1
PREPARATION: 5 MINUTES +
OVERNIGHT
COOK: 0 MINUTES

½ cup rolled (porridge) oats
1 teaspoon chia seeds
1¾ fl oz kefir milk
1 oz live yogurt (page 28)
1 teaspoon maple syrup, plus extra
   to serve
fruit, such as kiwi fruit and
   blueberries, to serve (optional)

Combine oats and chia seeds in a bowl. Add kefir, yogurt and maple syrup, stir to combine, cover and rest overnight in fridge. In morning, stir and serve with maple syrup and fresh fruit, if desired.

Lunch

GRILLED HALLOUMI & POMEGRANATE TABBOULEH

SERVES: 1
PREPARATION: 20 MINUTES
COOK: 5 MINUTES

1 oz bulgur wheat
grated zest and juice of ½ lemon
1 tablespoon extra virgin olive oil
1¾ oz canned garbanzo beans,
   drained and rinsed
1 tablespoon chopped parsley
1 tablespoon chopped mint
1 oz pomegranate seeds
3½ oz halloumi cheese, sliced
salt and pepper

Put the bulgur wheat into a heatproof bowl with 3½ fl oz boiling water, cover and leave for 15 minutes, or until tender. Drain and return to the bowl. Whisk lemon zest and juice with oil in another bowl and add to bulgur together with garbanzo beans, herbs and half the pomegranate seeds. Season with salt and pepper. Put a frying pan over medium heat and cook halloumi for 2 minutes on each side. Top tabbouleh with halloumi and sprinkle with remaining pomegranate seeds.

Dinner

LENTIL & GARBANZO BEAN BURGERS WITH CUCUMBER PICKLE

SERVES: 1
PREPARATION: 35 MINUTES
COOK: 8 MINUTES

7 oz canned mixed lentils and
   garbanzo beans, drained
   and rinsed
1 teaspoon ground turmeric
1 teaspoon chopped parsley
grated zest and juice of ½ lemon
1 egg
pinch of salt
¾ oz cornstarch
1 tablespoon rapeseed oil
2 tablespoons pickles, arugula
   and lemon wedge, to serve

Blitz pulses, turmeric, parsley, lemon zest and juice, egg and salt together in a food processor until smooth. Transfer to a bowl, mix in cornstarch and form into 2 burgers. Chill for 30 minutes. Heat oil in a large frying pan over medium heat and fry burgers for 4 minutes on each side, or until cooked. Serve with pickles, arugula and lemon wedge.

Easy Overnight Oats

*Grilled Halloumi &
Pomegranate Tabbouleh*

*Lentil & Garbanzo
Bean Burgers with
Cucumber Pickle*

Thursday

Fava beans are loaded with nutrients and are delicious prepared with vegetables in stews and soups. You can store the rest of the dinner in the fridge for another time.

Breakfast

BLUEBERRY & SPIRULINA SHAKE

SERVES: 1
PREPARATION: 5 MINUTES
COOK: 0 MINUTES

2¾ oz silken tofu, diced
⅓ cup blueberries
1 cup kefir milk
1 teaspoon maple syrup
1 teaspoon spirulina powder

Put all the ingredients into a blender and blitz until smooth. Serve.

Lunch

SEARED TUNA WITH CAPERS & OLIVE SALSA

SERVES: 1
PREPARATION: 5 MINUTES
COOK: 6 MINUTES

½ oz green olives, pitted and
   chopped
¼ oz salted capers, rinsed, drained
   and chopped
2 tablespoons extra virgin olive oil
1 teaspoon chopped parsley
1 teaspoon lemon juice
¼ teaspoon chili flakes
5½ oz tuna steak
salt and pepper

Combine the olives, capers, 1 tablespoon oil, parsley, lemon juice and chili in a large bowl and season to taste. Heat remaining oil in a non-stick frying pan and sear tuna steak for 3 minutes on each side or until cooked to your liking. Serve tuna with olive sauce.

Dinner

FAVA BEAN STEW

SERVES: 2
PREPARATION: 5 MINUTES +
OVERNIGHT
COOK: 45 MINUTES

5½ oz dried fava beans
2 tablespoons extra virgin olive oil
1 garlic clove, chopped
½ teaspoon chili flakes
7 oz rainbow chard, chopped
salt and pepper
1 slice sourdough bread, toasted,
   to serve

Soak fava beans in a bowl of water overnight. Next day, drain well, rinse and put into a large saucepan. Cover with water and cook for 30 minutes. Heat 1 tablespoon oil in a frying pan over medium heat and fry garlic and chili for 1 minute. Add to beans, then add chard and cook for 15 minutes, adding more water, if necessary. Season to taste, drizzle with remaining oil and serve with toasted bread.

Blueberry &
Spirulina Shake

Seared Tuna with
Capers & Olive Salsa

Fava Bean Stew

Friday

This dinner is so simple to make and is the best way to use any left-over pulses you have in your storecupboard, Store the rest of the soup in the fridge for another time.

Breakfast

OVERNIGHT QUINOA, OAT, APPLE & HAZELNUTS

SERVES: 1
PREPARATION: 5 MINUTES
+ OVERNIGHT
COOK: 0 MINUTES

1 oz quinoa, cooked
1½ oz rolled (porridge) oats
1 teaspoon honey
½ teaspoon ground cinnamon
1 cup milk of your choice
½ apple, unpeeled, cored and
   chopped
1 tablespoon hazelnuts, chopped

To a wide-mouth mason jar, add quinoa, oats, honey and cinnamon. Top with milk, stir to combine, then cover with lid and chill in fridge overnight. In the morning, stir well before adding apple and hazelnuts.

Lunch

TOFU SKEWERS & FREEKEH SALAD

SERVES: 1
PREPARATION: 35 MINUTES
COOK: 5 MINUTES

1 tablespoon triple nut butter
   (page 32)
½ teaspoon curry powder
3½ fl oz coconut milk
2¾ oz firm tofu, sliced into 1½ inch
   cubes
½ red bell pepper, sliced into
   1½ inch cubes
2¾ oz freekeh, cooked
1¾ oz mixed salad leaves

Mix butter, curry powder and coconut milk together thoroughly in a bowl. Stir in tofu and rest for 30 minutes. Remove tofu and thread onto metal skewers alternating with red pepper. In the bowl with left-over marinade, toss freekeh and salad leaves, then transfer to a plate. Heat a griddle pan over medium heat and cook tofu skewers for 2 minutes on each side. Serve on top of salad.

Dinner

MEDITERRANEAN SOUP

SERVES: 3
PREPARATION: 5 MINUTES
+ OVERNIGHT
COOK: 70 MINUTES

9 oz mixed dried beans such as
   cannellini and cranberry beans,
   lentils and garbanzo beans
1 tablespoon extra virgin olive oil,
   plus extra to drizzle
1 garlic clove, very finely chopped
2 cups vegetable stock
1 bouquet garni with thyme,
   rosemary, sage, bay leaves
salt and pepper
thyme sprigs, to garnish

Soak beans or pulses in a large bowl of cold water overnight. Next day, drain well and rinse. Heat oil in a large saucepan over medium heat and cook garlic for 1 minute. Add beans, stir, then cover with stock. Add bouquet garni, slowly bring to the boil, season to taste and simmer for about 1 hour, adding more stock, if necessary, until beans are soft. Once cooked, remove bouquet garni, drizzle with oil and garnish with thyme.

Overnight Quinoa, Oat, Apple & Hazelnuts

Tofu Skewers & Freekeh Salad

Mediterranean Soup

Saturday

Spelt is an ancient whole grain which contains a range of vitamins and minerals. It is also rich in fiber and is a hearty addition to the salad with its nutty, sweet flavor.

Breakfast

BREAKFAST BARS

SERVES: 1 / MAKES: 6
PREPARATION: 5 MINUTES
COOK: 35 MINUTES

5½ oz frozen mixed berries
3½ fl oz maple syrup
2 tablespoons chia seeds
1 egg
1¾ oz almond flour
⅓ cup whole-wheat flour
3 oz rolled (porridge) oats
2½ fl oz coconut oil, melted

Preheat oven to 350°F. Mix berries, 1 fl oz maple syrup, chia seeds and 1 tablespoon water in a saucepan and cook over medium heat for 5–8 minutes. Mix egg, flours, oats, coconut oil and remaining maple syrup together in a bowl. Set 1 oz of mixture aside, then spread rest in a lined 6 inch square baking tin. Cover with berry mix and sprinkle over reserved 1 oz oat mixture. Bake for 25 minutes, or until golden brown. Cool before cutting into 6 bars. Store in an airtight container in fridge for 2–3 days.

Lunch

CHARRED CHICKEN & KALE CAESAR SALAD

SERVES: 1
PREPARATION: 5 MINUTES
COOK: 25 MINUTES

2¾ oz sourdough bread, chopped
3 tablespoons extra virgin olive oil
¼ teaspoon sea salt
3 kale leaves, stems removed, leaves torn
3½ oz skinless, boneless chicken breast
½ garlic clove, mashed
1 oz live yogurt (page 28)
1 teaspoon Dijon mustard
½ oz shaved parmesan
salt and pepper

Preheat oven to 350°F. Toss bread with 1 tablespoon oil, sprinkle with salt, then spread out on a lined baking tray and bake for 10 minutes. Set aside. Put kale into a large bowl, drizzle with 1 tablespoon oil and season with salt and pepper. Arrange on a lined baking tray and bake for 15 minutes until crispy. Heat a frying pan over medium heat. Rub chicken with rest of oil, season and cook for 4 minutes on each side, or until fully cooked. Remove from pan, slice and set aside. For dressing, mix garlic, yogurt and mustard together in a bowl. Season. Arrange kale, chicken and crostini on a plate, drizzle with dressing and sprinkle parmesan over top.

Dinner

SPELT SALAD WITH RADICCHIO, CRANBERRY BEANS & TALEGGIO

SERVES: 1
PREPARATION: 5 MINUTES
COOK: 25 MINUTES

1 tablespoon butter
½ small red onion, chopped
2¾ oz spelt, rinsed
1 tablespoon white wine
10 fl oz boiling vegetable stock
1¾ oz canned cranberry beans, drained and rinsed
½ small radicchio, sliced
1 oz Taleggio cheese, chopped
salt and pepper

Heat butter in a saucepan over medium heat and cook onion for 3 minutes. Stir in spelt and toast for 1 minute, then add wine and simmer until evaporated. Cook spelt by adding a ladleful of boiling stock at a time and stirring frequently. After 15 minutes, add beans and radicchio and cook for another 5 minutes. Turn off heat, add Taleggio, season, stir and cover pan for 2–3 minutes before eating. Serve.

Breakfast Bars

Charred Chicken & Kale
Caesar Salad

Spelt Salad with
Radicchio, Cranberry
Beans & Taleggio

Sunday

This loaf for breakfast is soft, moist and flavorsome.
It is also perfect as an afternoon snack. You can store the
rest of the soup for lunch in the fridge for another time.

Breakfast

BANANA & MIXED SEED LOAF

SERVES: 1
PREPARATION: 5 MINUTES
COOK: 40 MINUTES

10½ oz spelt flour
1 teaspoon baking powder
1 tablespoon dark chocolate chips
7 oz mixed seeds
4 bananas, 3 mashed and 1 sliced
   lengthways
2¾ oz superfine sugar
⅓ cup rapeseed oil
2 eggs, lightly beaten
5½ oz Greek yogurt

Preheat oven to 350°F. Mix flour,
baking powder, chocolate chips
and 5½ oz mixed seeds together in
a large bowl. In another bowl, mix
mashed bananas, sugar, oil, eggs
and yogurt together. Add banana
mixture to dry ingredients and
mix well. Pour into a lined 8 x 4
x 3¼ inch loaf tin, sprinkle with
remaining seeds and put halved
banana on top. Bake for 40 minutes,
or until a skewer in center comes
out clean. Cool in tin for 5 minutes,
then transfer to a wire rack to cool
completely. Slice and store for
2–3 days.

Lunch

PROBIOTIC COLD GAZPACHO

SERVES: 2
PREPARATION: 5 MINUTES
COOK: 0 MINUTES

9 oz ripe tomatoes, halved, plus
   diced tomatoes, to garnish
½ red onion, finely diced
½ garlic clove, mashed
1 small cucumber
½ small red bell pepper
1 teaspoon apple cider vinegar
1 tablespoon extra virgin olive oil,
   plus extra for drizzling
¼ cup kefir milk
salt and pepper

Blitz tomato halves in a blender
for 30 seconds. Add remaining
ingredients and blitz to a thick
and smooth soup. Season and serve,
garnished with diced tomatoes and
drizzled with oil.

Dinner

CHILI SALMON NOODLES

SERVES: 1
PREPARATION: 5 MINUTES
COOK: 10 MINUTES

2 tablespoons soy sauce
2 tablespoons mirin
1 teaspoon chili sauce
1 salmon fillet, skin on
2½ oz buckwheat noodles
½ tablespoon sesame seeds
1 scallion, sliced

Mix soy sauce, mirin and chili
sauce together in a small bowl and
use half of mixture to coat salmon.
Heat a frying pan over medium heat
and cook salmon, skin-side down,
for 3 minutes, then turn over and
cook for another 1 minute. Remove
and keep warm. Meanwhile, cook
noodles in a large saucepan of
boiling water according to packet
instructions and drain well. Lightly
toast sesame seeds in frying pan
over medium heat for 3 minutes
until fragrant, add cooked noodles
with remaining sauce and toss
to mix. Serve with salmon
and scallion.

Banana & Mixed Seed Loaf

Probiotic Cold Gazpacho

Chili Salmon Noodles

Recipe index